MOTHERS AND DAUGHTERS MAKING PEACE

Mothers and Daughters Making Peace

The Most Intimate, Tangled, Beautiful, and Frustrating Relationship Shared by Women

Judith Balswick
with
Lynn Brookside

Servant Publications
Ann Arbor, Michigan

The names and characterizations in this book drawn from the author's case studies or her personal experience are rendered pseudonymously and as fictional composites. Any similarity between the names and characterizations of these individuals and real people is unintended and purely coincidental.

Vine Books is an imprint of Servant Publications especially designed to serve Evangelical Christians.

Published by Servant Publications
P.O. Box 8617
Ann Arbor, Michigan 48107

Cover photos and design by Michael Andaloro

93 94 95 96 97 10 9 8 7 6 5 4 3 2

Printed in the United States of America

ISBN 0-89283-781-0

Library of Congress Cataloging-in-Publication Data

Balswick, Judith K.
    Mothers and daughters making peace : the most intimate, tangled, beautiful, and frustrating relationship shared by women / Judith Balswick with Lynn Brookside
        p.   cm.
Includes bibliographical references.
ISBN 0-89283-781-0
1. Mothers and daughters.   2 Mothers and daughters—Case studies.   I. Brookside, Lynn.   II. Title.
HQ759.B266   1993
306.874'3—dc20   92-43413

Dedication

For
Agnes
&
Jacque

For My Daughter Angela

For generations they come
Like stair steps extending behind me.
Mother to my mother's mother and beyond
Stretching back to the earth itself.
Bringing me to this miracle—my child.

I hold her close and
Whisper to her of generations gone
And futures yet untold.
She clutches my finger
And drinks deeply of what only I can give her.

She sleeps and I watch
This little mystery-miracle
Too fascinated to sleep myself.
I dream instead of futures bold and promising.
Stretching in front of me.
Like stair steps.

—Lynn Brookside

Contents

Acknowledgments / 9

1. Your Mother's Indelible Imprint / 11
2. Generational Patterns: How They Shape Us / 25
3. Of Boundaries, Breakthroughs, and Mother-Bashing / 45
4. Bonding, Abandonment, Connection, and Love / 59
5. Mother, Do You Like Who I Am? / 75
6. Personality Traits and Mothering Styles / 99
7. The Circle of Love and Hate: What Happens with
   Unresolved Anger / 121
8. Conflict: How We Hate It! / 141
9. We Need to Be Influenced, Not Controlled / 163
10. Sex: Speaking the Unspoken Word / 181
11. When It's Time to Say Goodbye / 201
12. Making Peace with Your Mother / 217

Notes / 231
Bibliography / 235

Acknowledgments

THE VERY FIRST MOMENT editors Beth Feia and Ann Spangler planted the idea of this book in my heart and mind it took hold. They promised to guide me through the project and that's exactly what they did. It proved to be a challenging and stretching experience, and I am deeply appreciative for their encouragement and direction. I'm especially grateful for Beth's wise editorial counsel that helped shape and improve the book.

Lynn Brookside, my co-writer, painstakingly re-worked the rough edges, smoothed out the hard places, and added some wonderful pieces of herself. A talented and creative woman, Lynn made an enormous contribution to this book. She not only gave of herself with a loving spirit but proved to be a "soul-mate" and God-send.

It moves me deeply to think of the hallowed imprint so many women have made on my life. My mother, daughter, sister, grandmothers, aunts, cousins, nieces, sisters-in-law, mentors, students, clients, and friends have given of themselves, enriching and blessing me with their generosity. The intimacy that emerges out of our vulnerability, whether one on one or in a small group setting, proves to be the holy ground that leads us to personal wholeness.

It's with a great deal of joy that I also acknowledge the significant man in my life. Jack, my loving companion of thirty-three years has continuously empowered me to become all that God created me to be. This is undoubtedly an act of covenant love.

ONE

Your Mother's Indelible Imprint

"Not know your own mother?" cries Auntie An-mei with disbelief. *"How can you say that? Your mother is in your bones!"* [1]

THE ABSURDITY OF A daughter not knowing how deeply her mother lies within her is challenged by this character in Amy Tan's best-selling novel, *The Joy Luck Club*. To some extent, when we deny the effect our mothers have had in our lives, we deny ourselves. In order to understand who we are, we need to understand our mothers and their imprint on our lives.

For many of us, the very thought of our mothers stimulates a host of memories and feelings. The challenge of sorting out the complex dynamics of our mother-daughter relationships is well worth the effort. Exploring how that relationship has emerged, developed, and changed over the years requires careful and perhaps painful probing. In a few instances, the idea that a mother's imprint is in our bones may give rise to negative emotions. Some women might wish to deny the possibility that their mothers had anything whatsoever to do with who they are today. As painful as such thoughts may be, this book can be helpful to these women as well.

Only when we have come to peace with the part of us that we received from our mothers—for better or worse—can we come to a point of peace with ourselves and, ultimately, with our own daughters. For you whose relationship with your mother is particularly painful, I encourage you to take it slowly and ask a friend or therapist to help you work through some of your feelings. Such an exploration may reap even greater rewards for you in terms of self-knowledge and self-acceptance. Those who have suffered intense childhood abuse or neglect stand the chance of gaining greater peace of mind, growth, and healing.

NEVER NEUTRAL

Like it or not, we are profoundly influenced by our mothers throughout our lives. So much so, in fact, that it's nearly impossible to remain neutral about them. We love our mothers and desire their approval at one moment and are incensed and critical of them the next. A mother-daughter relationship is not only complex and multifaceted but also essential and profoundly influential.

Each daughter and mother is unique, and so is the relationship. Each mother-daughter pair lives with a different set of circumstances that determines their particular issues. In many cases, mothers and daughters will actually disagree about the events that shaped their relationship. Both have their own version of the same event and one may even seem to contradict the other. The truth is, both are correct. Both women have experienced the event from their own unique perspectives. Both carry their own impressions and emotion-laden memories. This book covers many significant aspects of the mother-daughter relationship, both the constructive and destructive facets, that I believe are fairly universal. I trust these will be informative and helpful, but I don't pretend to be able to exhaust the topic. I've drawn upon psychological and family systems material, as well as personal interviews with mothers and daughters of various ages, stages, and cultural perspectives. The practical exercises at the end of each chapter are designed to help you address your own issues in a more personal and action-oriented way.

I've written this book primarily for adult daughters who wish to have a better understanding of their mother-daughter relationship. Mothers who want to understand the imprint they've made on their daughters can also benefit from reading it. Perhaps you'll decide to explore your relationship by reading this book *with* your mother or daughter. Others may wish to use this book as an impetus for small group discussions.

I am convinced that daughters and mothers long to relate to one another in positive ways. Learning more about ourselves and this special relationship can help us find avenues that lead to health and wholeness in our lives. Such a challenging journey is well worth the effort. In most cases, the changes you wish to make in your relationships won't take place in the twinkling of an eye. But with time and through honesty, openness, understanding, and wisdom, change will come to pass.

As you contemplate your own story, my hope is that you will discover fresh insight that will strengthen the connection between you and your mother and/or daughter. Mutual understanding and peace come through *dialogue*. Uncovering our wounds and applying the healing salve of forgiveness and acceptance can bring restoration and intimacy.

I genuinely value the relationships I have with my own mother and daughter. Our journey in life has been one of joy and pain—never easy but always challenging! My mother is a jewel and we have remained closely connected for fifty-three years. My father refers to her as "precious," which captures my sentiments perfectly. My daughter and I continue to discover each other and grow in rewarding ways in our relationship. After twenty-nine years, we're more like friends now, reaping the benefits of mutual respect and love.

My mother-daughter relationships—in both directions—are and will always be an important part of my life. Both relationships have helped me to discover more about who I am. I thank both my mother and my daughter for letting me share some of our story in this book. In facing my reluctance to write about some of my own intimate memories, I have been struck with how private and personal our relationships are. Yet, having received their permission, I am also eager and proud to do so.

I could not write this book alone, however, because then it would simply be my own unique mother-daughter story. I've drawn upon the stories of acquaintances, friends, family members, and clients. I share their experiences in these pages with their consent. I have changed names and certain nonessential details in order to protect their identities. I remain deeply indebted to the women who have shared both the pain and pleasure of their personal mother-daughter stories. You will find them heart-rending, profoundly passionate, and intimate.

Many women have eagerly shared with me their personal reflections about their mother-daughter relationships. Each unique story provides examples of the ways in which our lives have been shaped by both painful and joyful experiences. The following statements came from five of the women who responded to my question, "How is your mother in your bones?"

Nancy: "My mother is deep within me and I can sense her vibrations even now as I speak of her. I even carry her body in mine. My thick knees are like hers. I carry the weight in my own body in the same places she carries hers. Sometimes I wonder if these extra pounds are a way of keeping her close to me. Having a similar body somehow means she is always with me."

Carol: "I watched her for years for clues as to how to become a woman. Is it any wonder that I come so close to being her clone, even though I was determined to do some things differently? When my husband calls me 'Evelyn' to remind me that I'm acting just like her, I'm rather shocked, but also amazed, by how much she is a part of me. I cook like she cooks, I clean my house like she cleans, I sound like her when I parent my kids, and I respond to my husband like she responds to my father."

Kim: "My mother was overly invested in my career successes and failures. It was as if she was living her life through me. I was also aware of her influence as I searched for spiritual truths about God. I began to recognize her in many aspects of my life and it was then that I realized how deeply she was embedded in my bones."

Emily: "I was like my mother, but my sister was just the opposite. She deliberately did things in reaction to her and they were in conflict through most of their relationship. I embraced her, while my sister rejected her. I gained weight, she lost; I attended church, she went to bars; I went to college, she barely made it through high school. Yet, we are both our mother's daughters. Mother is the focal point in determining our radically different behaviors. She impacted our lives in equally profound ways."

Maggie: "I thought I had freed myself of her when I became a sexual person and ventured into the world of love and passion. Yet, on dates I was constantly reminded of her spoken and unspoken messages about sex. When expressing my opinions, feelings, and values about sex in secret conversations with friends, I was aware of her influence. Even on my honeymoon, as I grappled with sexual inhibitions, her ghost seemed to appear."

Five different daughters with five different stories to tell, yet they all reflect a central theme: *our mothers leave an indelible imprint on our lives.* Do you see yourself in any of those descriptions? A mother's imprint is remarkably persistent, influencing the way we relate to others in obvious and not-so-obvious ways. Until we confront that unique influence in our lives, face-to-face, we can never fully know ourselves.

WILL MY REAL MOTHER PLEASE STAND UP?

One of the most important things we can do for ourselves as adult daughters is get to know our mothers as adult human beings—complete with character flaws and strengths—rather than the way we may have viewed them during our childhood or teens. Meeting our mothers as real persons forces us to be real with ourselves. Ferreting out some of the personal prejudices that color our maternal pictures can be challenging.

As we meet that challenge by questioning our biases, we may discover things we've kept hidden from ourselves. We may be obliged to give up an idealized view that keeps our mothers on a pedestal; we may have to let go of a contemptible view that keeps them forever condemned. Many of us have become so accustomed to seeing our mothers as the-one-who-is-meant-to-meet-our-needs that we haven't always been objective about who they are, completely separate from us, as people with lives of their own.

As mature adults, we have the opportunity and responsibility to step back for a moment and consider who our mothers really are. Unless we can approach them honestly, we will forfeit the possibility of a more grown-up perspective on this woman to whom we are tied by birth and shared history.

It may be scary when—like the old TV-game show—we ask our *real* mothers to stand up. We may find someone totally unexpected. Only when we honestly acknowledge this special individual in our lives can we transcend the false notions that continue to limit our understanding. Seeing our mothers clearly will make it much easier for us to decipher ways in which we have been shaped by them. And that, in turn, will give us the ability to make a healthy separation from our mothers so that we can take personal responsibility for who we are.

Discovering a mother's imprint can be a life-changing event. It was for Jan, a thirty-year-old who faced her mother's influence for the first time during one of her therapy sessions. This woman slumped in the baby-blue chair in my office, as if her bones had crumbled and no longer provided the structure to sit upright. Experiencing an almost overwhelming agony, Jan sobbed uncontrollably for several minutes. Exhausted and emotionally drained, she was finally able to talk about the neglect she had experienced as a child. As she spoke, I watched my client become energized by her rage.

"She was never there for me when I needed her! I had to go it alone and she never got it! She never understood that I needed her. **How could she have missed that?!** I ask myself over and over what I did wrong…. WHAT WAS WRONG WITH ME THAT SHE DIDN'T LOVE ME?"

It wasn't easy for Jan to express these powerful emotions after years of covering up for her mother, pretending that her childhood was perfect. Facing the truth about her mother's neglect was extremely difficult for Jan. That truth had been locked deep within her, waiting to explode for over thirty years. Exposing her wounds for the first time released the infection within and set into motion a healing process that changed my client's life in numerous ways.

Jan had tremendous problems relating to others in her adult life, but she had never connected her current difficulties with the events of her childhood. She had recently experienced more and more frequent eruptions of fury toward her husband. When he disappointed her, the molten mix of emotions from deep within her gut spewed out in his direction. Her volcanic blasts were confusing to him. Jan's anger flowed toward him like lava, destroying everything in its path, including their marriage. Until Jan exposed her wounds in my office that day, neither she nor her husband had ever suspected that her anger was really against her mother, deflected in his direction by her continuing need—a remnant from childhood—to pretend that Mommy was "perfect."

Unable to make up for the deficits of Jan's childhood, Bill began feeling like a failure as a husband. Sensing that a mere human could never fill the deep hole in Jan's heart—born of neglect and abandonment—he pulled away emotionally rather than allowing himself to fall in. His attempts to fill that hole dropped like mere pebbles into a chasm of neglect. Jan responded to his withdrawal with added anger and fear. She blamed herself for being a bad wife in the same way she had blamed herself for her childhood neglect, believing that it was her penalty for being a "bad child."

Then, gently and deliberately, Jan and I began the process of discovering the impact of her mother's neglect on her life. She learned to direct her legitimate, unexpressed anger toward her mother where it belonged. Eventually, this grown woman was able to shed her emotional burden by grieving the losses of her childhood. She began learning ways to nurture herself rather than blame herself. Jan learned to ask her husband and friends for what *she* needed, while recognizing and accepting the limits on what they could do for her. Most important, this adult daughter learned to trust.

Letting go of such a painful past wasn't easy. There are no instant cures to make up for serious deficits incurred during childhood. When Jan courageously addressed her mother's imprint, however, she was able to release her pain and find her own pathway to health.

Everyone in our lives suffers when we are at odds with our mothers, whether the difficulties are temporary or lifelong. If the problem has its roots in childhood, the resultant pain becomes an integral part of who we are. We can become so accustomed to that dull ache that we literally don't know how to exist without it. Many women expend a great deal of time and energy focused on old, self-defeating patterns that keep them stuck in intolerable and untenable situations. Facing the pain and letting go allows us to recover and change.

Gerry had a very different experience when she began to face her mother's imprint on her life. Gerry's mom, Helen, had grown up in a very artistic family. Helen spent hundreds of hours in community theatre and musical productions as a teenager and continued to appear in local productions even as an adult. Gerry remembers Helen as a beautiful, vivacious woman who seemed to attract attention wherever she went.

Gerry adored watching her mother's rehearsals and dreamed of being in the spotlight herself one day. And Helen encouraged Gerry to study music and to audition for children's theatre productions. But Gerry balked at her mother's suggestions because she didn't believe she could ever compete with her mother's local fame. She allowed her dream of acting and singing to lie fallow rather than risk failing at something that seemed to come so easily to her mother.

After completing a seminar on the mother-daughter relationship, Gerry visited her parents' home and talked frankly with her mother about her childhood memories of "never being good enough." Gerry described the event in this way:

"I'd finally said it. It was finally out in the open—my jealousy of my mother. Mom was dumbfounded. She had never realized that I had felt that way. She gently reminded me of all the times she had encouraged me to try my hand at acting and music. She talked about the little part she got for me when the adult theatre needed a couple of kids for a show they were doing. She told me how proud she was of the great job I did. I told her I had felt that it didn't count since I was only cast in the role because I was her daughter.

"Mom said, 'You may have gotten the role because you were my daughter, but you did a superb job because you're Gerry: a very talented person in your own right. I kept encouraging you to try another role because I always suspected that you had far more talent than I ever dreamed of having. I was merely good. I think you could have been truly wonderful.'

"And there it was. My mother had always believed in me. I had simply been too afraid to try stepping out of her shadow. When I got back home I called the community theatre here in our town. I'm just getting my feet wet... trying little odd jobs backstage. But I love it! And next season they're doing a show I've always adored. I'm going to audition. What can it hurt?"

No doubt about it, our mothers wield tremendous influence on our lives—and we on theirs. Perhaps that's why we have such a difficult time when things go wrong between our mothers and ourselves. An objective and systematic exploration of this emotion-laden bond can easily elude our best efforts. Even after we have worked to discover our mothers' imprint, transforming those insights into the desired changes can seem utterly impossible. This book is meant to guide you in your process of discovery and to provide a source of encouragement, healing, and renewal as you travel this difficult road.

REFLECTION AND JOURNALING

Unconditional love, acceptance, empowerment, and intimacy are the building blocks that make up all healthy relationships. When one or more of these relational building blocks is weak or lacking, our interconnections begin to list and crumble. We learn from our earliest bonding, usually with our mothers, how to utilize those building blocks. If that foundational experience failed to teach us how to utilize these building blocks, then we must play catch-up later in life if we're ever to enjoy the benefits of healthy interconnectedness with others.

Most of us would like to work toward improving relationships with the significant people in our lives. Leaving important issues unexamined or unresolved can cause disruptions in our relationships, which in turn disrupts our own lives in various ways. Sometimes we err in the direction of keeping peace at all costs, failing to confront, ignoring our feelings because we fear that tampering with the relationship will be destructive. Sometimes, in our eagerness to work things out, we can actually drive our loved ones further from us or push them into a defensive stance.

When we neglect to examine our relationships—whether out of fear or frustration or anger—we allow our wounds to remain unhealed and they continue to fester. Being open and self-reflective allows us to honestly face both the joyous and sorrowful elements of our mother-daughter relationship, including issues that we may have put off facing because they appear too difficult or painful to change. The questions at the end of this chapter can help you to identify your own personal goals with respect to this foundational relationship.

Writing your thoughts and responses to these questions in a personal journal can be especially helpful. I suggest you commit yourself to a short period of time each day—perhaps ten or fifteen minutes—to reflect on your relationship with your mother. Such a deliberate pace can allow you to examine an intense relationship in small segments without feeling overwhelmed.

During this time of reflection, write down any thoughts, feelings, or memories that come to mind. Events from your past will eventually help you see the bigger picture. The process may seem a bit fragmented in the beginning, but as you continue with your work you'll begin to see how the themes and patterns of the puzzle come together to form a whole.

You may find it helpful to pretend that your mother is in the room with you so you can talk directly to her. Don't be afraid to shout out your love or anger or fear or frustration, or close your eyes and speak quietly to her as you envision her in the room. You may even want to imagine how your mother would respond so that you can enter into a sort of dialogue. These heart-to-heart "talks" can begin to heal the wounds of the past even when she's not actually there with you.

A private time of reflection may actually free you to express things you've never been able to say to your mother. Feelings of joy, anger, sadness, and frustration will probably surface. I encourage you to give yourself permission to acknowledge and embrace the full range of your emotions. Doing so will provide you a catharsis. Then, at some later time, you may decide to express some of your thoughts and feelings to your mother, face-to-face.

It may be especially helpful for you to have a friend or small group to help you work through this book, particularly if you have a stormy mother-daughter relationship. A group of trusted friends provides a safe context in which you can examine your own personal issues. Sharing with each other will give you a helpful perspective and increase your own insights as you learn from one anothers' thoughts and experiences. Besides offering a listening ear and emotional support, such a group can also help you practice new ways of relating to your mother.

Change for the better is the ultimate goal. This begins to happen when we transform our personal insights into deliberate actions. New behavior will lead to changes in attitude, just as changes in our attitude will give us the ability to make needed changes in our behavior. With this in mind, I've written this book as a step-by-step process, using each chapter to focus on one particular dimension of the mother-daughter relationship.

My hope is that your journey will help you uncover both the joys and sorrows deep within you as a result of the impact your mother has had—and may still be having—on your life. Investigate this unique relationship at whatever pace feels comfortable. May this book challenge you to become more aware of your interactional patterns, to gain new insights about your relationship, to acknowledge, express, and heal the pain from your past—as well as to recognize all the good that your mother has brought into your life. May you find greater hope for future changes that will serve to strengthen, repair, and restore one of the most intimate, tangled, beautiful, and frustrating relationships shared by women.

I believe we are created in the image of God and valuable to God, who is the hope and sustainer of all life and relationships. I also believe that we are empowered, through the Holy Spirit, to live our lives in committed love and forgiving grace. It is to that end, and in God's service, that I have written this book. May you read it in the same spirit.

Exercises

1. How would you describe yourself to a group of trusted friends? How would you describe your mother to this same group? What are the similarities and differences?

2. Describe yourself as you think your mother would describe you. Is there any difference in this description and the way you just described yourself? What differences do you see in either of these portraits and the way the Bible describes you as a child of God?

3. Describe your relationship with your mother. What feelings surface when you reflect on your relationship?

4. How well do you know your mother? How well do you think she knows you? What are some of the secrets about yourself that you have never shared with her? Why?

5. How has your relationship with your mother changed over the years? How have these changes occurred? Is there something more you want to change about yourself in that relationship? How are you going to make it happen?

6. List three specific goals you would like to achieve in improving your relationship with your mother.

TWO

Generational Patterns: How They Shape Us

"I am walking down a long stretch of beach with my mother and my daughters. I walk between them, linking generations. It is one of those cool, clear, winter days that blesses the northern coast of California. Sea and sky are vivid blue. There is a light wind and someone thinks she sees whales out there. I can't remember what we are talking about, but I do remember a surge of feeling that goes beyond words—a wave of overarching connections, of the present moment holding within it the seeds of both past and future, and all of it held in the bodies of these four women of three generations."[1]

EACH OF US FORMS AN ESSENTIAL link between the generations of women in our family line. God established families as a way to continue this biological and cultural heritage. Rooted in the genes of our parents, every daughter contains her mother and her mother's mother, and on and on,extending back farther than recorded history. And our wombs hold the hope of future generations to come.

If we are ever to truly understand ourselves, we need to know where we fit within this bigger picture.

Many of us demonstrate loyalty to our family heritage in the rituals we pass from generation to generation. Most of us cook special holiday foods much like our mothers did. I may not like the traditional Swedish dinner and the smell of fish may drive my kids crazy, but I carry on the tradition nevertheless as a symbol of my own heritage.

One year my nine-year-old daughter was upset because I didn't bake the coconut-covered bunny cake for Easter. Another year Christmas felt somehow incomplete because I never finished the traditional batch of homemade candy. Such personal memories convince me of the importance of family traditions. Even when these ways of celebrating become modified over the years, our emotional attachment can remain intact. A complete lack of family traditions leaves the next generation feeling rootless. Understanding our mother-daughter relationship in the context of our generational heritage is essential.

ONE PLUS ONE DOESN'T NECESSARILY EQUAL TWO

In the days following birth, members of the extended family gather around the newborn infant, oohing and aahing over this latest addition. "Who does she look like? Will her eyes be blue or brown? Which side of the family does she favor?" Sometimes each individual seems to be jockeying for position, hoping to see a little bit of themselves reflected in the rapidly changing baby. Often both sides of the family claim this little one as their own, perhaps to strengthen their own position within the family.

Our lives form a delicate tapestry, interwoven with the biological strands, the cultural textures, and historical colors of our family's heritage. You are more than your mother's daughter; you are also the daughter of your mother's extended family system. You may be oblivious to this fact at birth, but it won't be long before you feel the family influence. Carl Whitaker expressed his firm conviction that we're shaped by our family system in this way: "There are no individuals. Everyone is a fragment of their family."[2]

Babies have a marvelous habit of wriggling their way into a mother's heart. They're soft, vulnerable little people who easily captivate and command love. They shape a mother's life, just as she shapes theirs. The beliefs and assumptions of extended family members also shape this newborn infant. In my family, for example, women are viewed as strong. My mother and her sisters managed to survive a harsh world with little education, working hard to keep their family together after the untimely death of their father. These women served as important role models for me.

I became aware, at an early age, that I was expected to carry on this tradition of feminine strength. Such family beliefs are passed down through the generations, tacitly or otherwise, starting with the newest family member. When a baby girl grows up being valued as a female by her family, she will grow up believing she is worthwhile and has an important contribution to make to the larger world.

Do you have any symbols of your own family heritage? My Grandma Nelson's sugar bowl sits on my kitchen table to remind me of my Swedish roots. A small, humble woman, my father's mother radiated a huge capacity for love and empathy. I remember how she took my hands in hers and washed them in the kitchen sink. Her gentle, warm qualities helped to shape my life. How many times I sat at Grandma Nelson's kitchen table watching her cook. Even now, when I think of her, I can almost smell the Swedish pancakes and taste the whipped butter mixed with the sugar that came from that very same sugar bowl. Attending the Lutheran church each Sunday and having dinner at Grandpa and Grandma's house were weekly rituals.

My mom's mother evokes sweet memories as well. A proud Dutch woman who had been widowed for years, Grandma Rummelt lived in a small trailer next to our large farmhouse. We children used to refer to her as "the peacock" behind her back because she seemed so proud. Yet, Grandma Rummelt introduced me to the beauty of created things. Going with her on walks to pick the wild flowers in the wheat fields remains one of my favorite memories. We would end up in her cozy little trailer, eating cookie sandwiches. Grandma would drink coffee while mixing equal portions of coffee and milk for me. She was a woman of strong character and mind, a teacher who read her Scofield Bible to me and passed on her reformed theology.

Both of my grandmothers left a profound imprint on my life. Grandmother Nelson's warmth and empathy come into play as I hug my own daughter and counsel clients; Grandmother Rummelt's strength and creativity shape my family activities and personal projects. These vital links with my heritage remind me that I am never alone: I am a member of a much larger community.

Where the family is concerned, the whole is greater than the sum of the individual parts. The idea that one person *acts* and another *reacts* doesn't tell the whole story. We can't explain the dynamics between mother and daughter simply by adding one mother plus one daughter. Their interaction must be viewed as an integral part of a much larger family system before we can fully understand it.

Imagine a butterfly mobile hanging over a baby's crib and think about how it moves. We see one entity, the mobile, that's made up of several interacting parts. Each separate piece activates another, causing movement in the whole. You can't determine which part *started* the movement, because each single piece influences and is being influenced by every other piece at the same time. That's the way families work, like a constantly shifting mobile.

Gretchen's recollection of her breastfeeding experience with her second child is a perfect example of this principle. She had been unable to breastfeed her first child, who was two years old when she gave birth to her second. Gretchen was determined to breastfeed successfully this time, but felt a bit awkward and unsure of how to go about it. The baby seemed disinterested, crying and turning away from the breast. The emotionally invested mother felt rejected, wondering if something was wrong with her or her milk. Gretchen's newborn picked up on the mother's emotional stress, which increased the baby's fussiness, contributing further to the negative nursing experience.

Not only do mother and daughter individually play a part in the interaction but also the combined pair contributes a third part: the interaction between the two. An objective observer would probably be more aware of this third piece of the puzzle than of either individual's singular contribution.

In addition to all that was occurring between mother and baby, however, other family members offered important input to this whole drama. Gretchen's husband was sitting only a few feet away from her reading the newspaper while his wife struggled to nurse the baby. Their two-year-old, naturally feeling jealous and left out, was simultaneously hanging onto one of her mother's legs.

The extended family entered into this domestic scene as well. Gretchen's mother, who had come to help out for the first few weeks of the new baby's life, was on the phone asking advice of Gretchen's older sister, who had successfully breastfed both of her children. Grandma felt that asking her advice seemed a reasonable thing to do. And it might have been, if Gretchen hadn't grown up feeling that her sister "always did everything right," while she herself struggled along trying "just to keep it together."

Gretchen's mental and emotional state was further aggravated by many other less tangible factors: her husband's seeming lack of interest; her concern for and frustration with her two-year-old; her more pervasive feelings of inferiority; her feeling of betrayal that her mother was telling her sister about "yet another failure" in her life. Is it any wonder that mother and baby were off to a rough start?

Mother-daughter interactions would be very complex even if the two individuals formed only an isolated pair. But when additional family members are factored into this mix, it becomes even more volatile. Each person and his or her interactions must be taken into account in order to understand the entire *family system*. But the nuclear family of parents and siblings seldom stands alone. When you consider the contributions of the extended family and other community members, the brew becomes still more complex. All of these individuals, plus the interactions between them, make up the complex dynamics of any family system.

OH, YOU BEAUTIFUL DOLL

Family relationships can be compared with the wooden Russian dolls that nest one inside the other. Beginning from the inner core and continuing outward, we can see a hierarchy of sorts. The central doll represents the individual person. The second layer represents the immediate nuclear family, which itself includes various sub-systems (spousal, parental, and sibling). Third comes the extended family of grandparents, aunts, uncles, and cousins. The fourth largest doll represents the social system (church, neighborhood, and school). Finally, society, world, and universe systems encompass all these smaller human layers.

Every baby exerts a powerful effect on the mother, thereby

causing vibrations in every other part of the immediate and extended family as well. The older brother has a new sister; the mother's sister has a new niece; the grandparents have a new grandchild; the church has a new member; the neighborhood has a new neighbor. We're influenced at every level of our being by all the levels of our society and we in turn influence our society at every level. The ripples extend in all directions beginning at our births, sometimes even conception, and go on for the span of our lifetimes and beyond.

In the case of Gretchen's struggle with breastfeeding, we must consider what is happening in other family relationships in order to get a complete picture. What might the husband's role be in this scenario? He could assure his wife of her adequacy and relieve her of some of the overload by comforting their two-year-old. Or he could throw up his hands in apparent defeat and offer to run to the store for formula, thereby validating his wife's deepest fears of inadequacy.

What about the extended family? Of course, Gretchen's mother was trying to lend support. At least she didn't undermine her adult daughter with horror stories of her own failed nursing experiences. But the grandmother might have been a greater help if she had offered to entertain her two-year-old grandson or simply shared some affirming comments with her daughter. Familial support systems can make a crucial difference to both mother and daughter.

But we can look to yet a larger picture. A sociologist, for example, might direct our attention to the hospital. Did they have a trained staff to instruct the mother so that mother and baby started out with a positive interaction? Every level within the hierarchy that makes up our society influences the outcome of our relationships.

It's impossible to determine where a problem starts or stops. Basically, it's the old chicken and egg question. A problem that develops within a family creates a sort of loop that feeds into itself. Did the mother's anxiety cause the baby to refuse to nurse or did the baby's fussiness cause the mother's anxiety?

If our thinking were linear, we might decide that the baby caused the problem because she wouldn't eat. By extension then, we might decide that, in order to solve the problem, we must figure out what's wrong with the baby and treat that symptom, possibly by helping her to burp. A different linear interpretation would be to blame the mother for responding immaturely when the baby refused to eat. The way to solve the problem, in this case, would be to fix the mother.

With a more flexible approach, however, we might assume that the transactions between mother and daughter play a significant part as well. The initial negative interaction sets up the possibility that mother and baby will anticipate a repeat of the frustration. That then becomes part of the problem. So, round and round it goes; where it stops, nobody knows.

Early mother-daughter encounters have an impact on future interactions. A client of mine heard the "diaper-pin story" from her mother many times as a child. The fact that Renee heard this story retold so often indicated just how important the incident seemed in the eyes of her mother. When she was just five months old, her mother left Renee for a moment on the changing table. During her mother's absence the baby swallowed a diaper pin.

When her mother returned, Renee was literally choking to death. Her mother panicked and ran out of the house screaming for help. Fortunately, a neighbor heard her and came running. He sent Renee's mother to the basement for a pair of pliers, but while she was gone he reached into the baby's throat with his fingers and retrieved the pin, saving her life.

No one blamed Renee's mother for the near tragedy, but knowing how close her daughter had come to death through her own carelessness caused her to feel tremendous guilt. In response to the nearly tragic event, the mother became overprotective. Despite the fact that she had other children, she coddled and favored Renee constantly. Her brother and sister resented the special attention she received and created a coalition against her. Her father seemed to be on the outside of this intense mother-daughter relationship, which prevented Renee from ever really feeling close to him.

That single incident helped to shape both their mother-daughter dynamics as well as the family dynamics. It wasn't until recently, at a family gathering, that they were able to talk together about the impact of that particular incident on their relationships. Renee felt a sense of relief after talking to her siblings about their reactions. She hoped it would give them an opportunity to begin to respond more positively to her in the future.

GENERATIONAL PATTERNS

Rather than being the result of a single, nearly tragic incident, Teri's dysfunctional pattern of communication with her mother portrayed a generational pattern. She finally recognized the pattern after taking a walk around the block with her mother early one evening. As they stopped to watch the sun dip below the mountaintops, her mother asked, "Aren't you chilly, Teri?"

Teri immediately put her arm around her mother to warm her up. It was an automatic response to her mother's query. Teri knew, intuitively, that her mother was asking the question on her own behalf rather than out of concern for her daughter. Years of conditioning had triggered the response her mother was fishing for, although an outsider might have been puzzled by Teri's automatic action.

When they had returned home, Teri noticed a sick feeling in the pit of her stomach. She felt irritable, guilty, and extremely angry with her mother, but couldn't put her finger on the reason. At first Teri concluded that something must be wrong with *her*. Yet, she sensed that it had to do with the interaction between her and her mother. She became sure when she realized that just recalling the incident made her shudder. What was going on here? she wondered.

After her mother left, Teri reflected on what had happened. Going over it step-by-step, she realized that she had automatically responded to a stimulus that had become all too familiar. Rather than asking directly for what she needed, Teri's mother had indirectly telegraphed her need to her daughter. The well choreographed dance flowed so smoothly that neither of them faltered a step. Yet, Teri's stomach indicated her discomfort. Her deep-seated emotional response told her something was radically wrong with the encounter.

As Teri mentally sorted through past interactions with her mother, going back to early childhood, she began to see just how commonplace these automatic interactions had become. Over the next few days, the emptiness and unreality of her relationship with her mother became more clearly focused in her mind.

It wasn't that her mother never tried to meet Teri's needs. She did. Teri wasn't feeling cheated; she was feeling used and deceived. Why couldn't her mother simply ask, outright, for what she needed? Why wouldn't she be honest and say that she wanted to be hugged or kept warm? Instead, she manipulated her daughter into giving her something under the pretense that it was for Teri's good. Teri had to admit that her mother wasn't manipulating her consciously. Her mother had even deceived herself into believing that she was meeting her daughter's needs rather than her own.

Teri wondered how such confusion could have developed. She had to go back to her mother's mother for some clues. That's when Teri discovered that she and her mother were hapless victims of a family myth. She found that her mother's family myth stated that females should not have needs, and since they have no needs, they certainly must never ask to have their needs met. As a girl, Teri's mother never felt she had permission to express her own needs, so she had to pretend she had none. As an adult, the only way she could give herself permission to have her own needs met was to do so in the guise of meeting her children's needs.

Can you see how deviously and unconsciously such a subterfuge can develop? A mother can get hugs by hugging her children, even when they don't wish to be hugged. A mother can be the center of her children's universe by making herself indispensable to them, by waiting on them so that they never learn to do for themselves. We even reward mothers who sacrifice themselves for their own children... even when it's really at the children's expense. Daughters are frequently deemed the perfect recipients of these unwanted attentions since they're *supposed* to be dependent and needy.

Teri felt a deep sadness for her mother. But she found it difficult to reconcile her sadness with the anger she still felt. Watching her aunts and grandmother, Teri realized that this family myth was well ingrained. "Women had no needs; women existed only to meet the needs of others; having or expressing needs was selfish and self-centered." Teri remembered her mother frequently saying that J-O-Y stood for "Jesus," "others," and "yourself"—in that particular order of importance. But it wasn't until then that Teri realized the immense personal and emotional significance of her mother's definition.

While it's true that we do find deep joy in giving to others, our lives become riddled with half-truths when we deny our own needs in order to do so. Teri's mother was telling only half the truth when she inquired about whether her daughter was cold. Having long repressed any consciousness of her own needs, she was no longer even aware of them. She allowed herself to see only the half of the truth that she deemed acceptable: her concern for Teri.

Teri felt caught in a trap of dishonesty. She described herself as "the pawn who must serve the queen." She felt used and misused by her mother, yet felt guilty when she didn't give her mother what she couldn't ask for directly. Eventually Teri realized that when the giving is done reluctantly, it fails to really satisfy the need anyway.

Teri believed that she and her mother couldn't talk openly about their family myth without blowing her mother's cover. She was worried that her mother wouldn't be able to deal with the truth, so she felt she was left with no alternative but to continue to play the game and perpetuate the family myth. Continuing the pattern took a serious toll on Teri and on the relationship. Teri sought more and more distance from her mother. Her mother, sensing that her daughter was moving away from her, clung all the more desperately when Teri was with her.

But it didn't end just with that single mother-daughter relationship. Teri had difficulty admitting her own needs to other family members as well. As the oldest daughter she was saddled with the responsibility of caring for her mother's needs. Teri was frustrated and resentful of her grown siblings, who didn't seem to be taking their fair share of the responsibility. At the same time, she had to admit that they had no way of knowing that she wanted their help, that she wanted things to change. Teri felt trapped in a "no win" situation.

Teri began to realize that her inability to admit to having needs helped to explain her difficulty in being herself around her friends and colleagues. Why was she so alert to everybody else's needs and oblivious to her own? Why didn't she dare ask for anything for herself? Teri decided that unless she found a way out of this family trap she would perpetuate this myth when she had children of her own. That thought caused her no small discomfort.

After finding a therapist to help her deal with her confusion, Teri listened as her therapist told her gently and repeatedly that it's okay to have needs. Gradually she learned to test that premise with her therapist, sometimes asking for a hug or feedback of a particular kind. She started to take risks with others as well. Teri began to trust some of her friends to help her out once in a while. Once she was able to recognize and admit her own needs, Teri began to find ways to meet her needs for herself, to nurture herself in various ways. Best of all, she began to admit her needs to God and look to him to satisfy those deepest needs.

It took time for Teri to learn to trust. It was scary to be honest with her therapist and friends about her real feelings because doing so made her feel so vulnerable. She tested her therapist; she tested her friends; she tested herself. And she grew.

One day Teri began to wonder when she might have the courage to break some of the old patterns with her mother. Her therapist had explained that one person's change alters the relationship and the resulting ripples then spread throughout the family. Teri wondered whether she dared enlist the aid of her brother and sister in making necessary changes. Maybe, together, they could find ways to give their mother what she needed in more direct and honest ways.

Breaking the silence and openly recognizing the family myth was the beginning of change for Teri, her mother, and their entire family system. It usually happens in such small but significant steps. Taking the risk was well worth the effort.

All families pass on myths of some sort. Since they characteristically hold some degree of truth, it isn't always easy to determine what our family's myths are and whether they're helpful or harmful. These underlying beliefs aren't necessarily destructive. My own family's myth—that all women are always strong—proved to be an encouragement to me. If it had been passed on to me in an exaggerated form or as a rigid rule to obey, it might have prevented me from admitting my occasional need for assistance or encouragement. Fortunately, my family's myth left adequate room for individual needs and foibles.

A heightened expectation of strength could also have worked against me if I had been born in poor health. In that case I might have felt that I was being held up to a standard I couldn't meet. That could have caused me to feel like a failure as a woman. Or it could have worked against me if some new twist had been added to my family's myth. If my mother had taught me that women are strong and men are incompetent dimwits, that would probably have worked against me in my selection of a mate. I might have been unconsciously programmed to seek a "dimwit" to marry. Fortunately, I was helped rather than hindered by my family's myth.

Some families pass on the myth that "members of our family are *never* sick," and they actually do tend toward heartiness and good health. Such a positive mental attitude about one's health might also work against someone, however. In my own case, that family's myth would likely lull me into neglecting warning signs about my health, signs that would cause another person to seek a physician's help in time to avert a disaster. Being aware of our family's myths usually proves helpful, if for no other reason than to make us more watchful for the inherent pitfalls of even the most positive beliefs.

SETTING CHANGE INTO MOTION

Most of us prefer that things remain the same. We feel more secure when our lives are relatively stable. But because we live in a world that's constantly changing and demanding that we change with it, our desire for a predictable existence can present serious problems. Typically, families attempt to maintain stability by being resistant to change. Even when generational patterns are obviously unhealthy, many people tend to prefer them because they are at least familiar. Often, we don't know how to step outside the limits of our established patterns. We keep doing things the same old way, rather than seeking alternatives. We are frequently unaware that alternatives even exist.

So how does change occur? I can offer no simple answer to that question, but one thing is clear: when one family member changes, it eventually affects the entire family. Remember the mobile above the baby's bed? Movement or change in one part automatically affects movement in the other parts and in the whole. Overall change is inevitable. Even a simple change in one relationship is often enough to set into motion a change in the whole family.

It's the brave one—perhaps the family member who has been designated as "troubled"—who often gets the change started. And it's usually the most sensitive member of the family who acts out her personal pain as a means of pointing out the pain suffered by the entire family. It's as if that person were saying, "I'm hurting because we're all hurting. Let's get help!"

Alison came to therapy because she was concerned about her children, Jason, Robert, and her nine-year-old daughter, Stephanie. Once the family was in therapy it became obvious that Stephanie was asking for a closer relationship with her mother. But Alison seemed resistant to the kind of closeness her daughter seemed to need.

One evening in my office I asked Alison and Stephanie to talk to one another about their relationship. Soon, this mother and daughter were stuck again, having encountered the same impasse they had encountered a hundred times before in their relationship. I didn't have a clue as to how this sad pattern could be broken. Alison seemed paralyzed by the very thought of getting close to her daughter.

Alison's mother, Jean, had died five years earlier. It happened that Aunt Jane, her mother's twin sister, was scheduled to visit the following week. I asked Alison to invite Aunt Jane to join us during our next appointment. During that session, when Stephanie made another attempt to get close to her mother, Alison literally pulled her chair back an inch or two. Stephanie assumed that she had done something "bad" and tears sprang to her eyes. We all sat there in awkward silence.

Then Aunt Jane began to speak, recounting stories about her grandfather's sexual and physical abuse of his granddaughter. Jane spoke of the times that she and Alison's mother, Jean, had been abused. The family listened intently, sharing her pain. When Aunt Jane was finished there was a moment of silence.

Then Alison began to speak, recounting the times she had been abused as a child. She described how Jean had once deliberately burned her arm with a hot iron. Alison grabbed her arm as if the wound still ached. Now, for the first time, she was able to express the anger and hurt she felt about the incident. We listened as she poured out her anguish, voicing her fear that she might do the same thing to her own daughter.

Finally, Alison turned to Stephanie and confessed that this was the reason she pulled away when Stephanie attempted to get close. Alison feared closeness with her own daughter because she thought she might become abusive. As long as she remained detached, she felt she could control those impulses. Stephanie softened toward her mother, relieved to know the distance between them was founded in her mother's fear. Until then Stephanie had assumed—as children so often do—that she simply didn't merit her mother's love and attention.

The sins of our fathers and mothers are often passed from generation to generation. In this particular family, the abusive relationships of the past were harming innocent victims in the present. But here was a chance to break the cycle of abuse. Their new understanding seemed to empower this family to pursue change. Aunt Jane imparted hope to Alison by describing the way she had broken the pattern in her own family. Jane pleaded, "You don't have to carry the abuse any farther. The buck can stop with you! It has stopped with me in my home, and I will support you so it will stop in your home as well."

The pain of the past had been exposed. Old, unhealthy patterns had been challenged. Because one person had demonstrated the courage to change things for herself, another generation was being infused with that same courage so that future generations could be set free. Having taken such a giant leap forward, this family continued in therapy and began to engage each other emotionally.

Alison gained confidence in her ability to deal with her anger in safe, constructive ways. Aunt Jane helped her niece find someone to babysit one night a week so that Alison could attend group meetings which addressed the complex issues that had stemmed from her childhood abuse. Jane also called Alison frequently to encourage her and lend moral support. Because of her aunt's example, Alison learned that change within her own family could begin with her. She took pride in the fact that she was whittling away the foundation of those destructive patterns she might otherwise have passed on to future generations.

ONE SMALL STEP FOR WOMANKIND

It takes courage to be the one to blow the whistle on the family. It's risky to disrupt the status quo by pointing out the myths and habits that perpetuate unhealthy patterns. Those who are afraid to make waves actually enable the system to continue its dysfunctional ways. If change doesn't begin with us, perhaps it won't begin at all.

Taking that first step toward change will doubtless be disruptive. Family members may start clamoring for old familiar patterns. They may even point the finger at you for being a troublemaker. But a dysfunctional system needs to be challenged so that healthy patterns can be established and passed on to future generations.

I remember the day I risked change by deciding not to attend a Christmas celebration. Many family members didn't appreciate my decision, but I was amazed to find that they were able to get along just fine without me there to play my part. Like pieces of the baby's mobile, other family members moved in to fill the opening left by my absence. My courage to change allowed my sister to take a more significant role. It also broke me out of my need to be needed and to control what happened at family gatherings.

My absence at the Christmas celebration accomplished its intended purpose: it removed me from the loop created by some of the old patterns in my family, so that when I returned I could relate to them more positively. My action seemed pretty scary and I caught some flack for being disruptive. But when I was willing to change my role in the system, the entire system made needed changes as well. All of our family members and their interactions are healthier as a result.

I encourage you to take the same kind of risk. Try to discover the ways in which the dynamics of your extended family may have affected your relationship with your mother. Try to determine ways you can change the interactions between you and your mother and other family members. Start with just one, small, achievable step and see how it affects your relationships.

In addition, you might want to investigate the probability that your family has passed on myths that you and your mother have believed. Try to define those family myths. If possible, talk them over with your mother. You may find that she is ready to set them aside or at least assess their good and bad points along with you.

Also, try to think of something affirming that you are willing to do for your mother. Take your mother by surprise by starting a new pattern of interaction as well as changing an unhealthy one from the past. Use the exercises in this book to get you started. Find someone you can talk to about the change you want to make and ask them to support you as you carry out your decision.

Exercises

1. What action would you be willing to take to change an unhealthy pattern in your mother-daughter relationship? Make a point to do it as often as you can when you're together.

2. In what ways did your grandmothers or other family members help to shape your values and expectations of life? To help you appreciate your family heritage, try to spend some time delving into your family history.

3. What family myths can you identify, especially ones that relate to being a woman? What are women in your family expected to be and do?

4. What are the positive and negative aspects of those family myths? What is there in each myth for which you can be thankful? In what ways do you need to be more cautious in order not to be tripped up by the down side of the myth?

5. Ask God to show you concrete ways to alter any negative aspects of your family myths. How can they be more fully aligned with what the Scriptures indicate about the family of believers to which you now belong?

THREE

Of Boundaries, Breakthroughs, and Mother-Bashing

*"A son is a son 'til he takes a wife,
a daughter is a daughter for the rest of her life."*

MOST CULTURES IMPART THE MESSAGE—spoken or unspoken—that daughters are forever responsible for their mothers. But the task of being forever responsible for *anyone* is likely to become overwhelming even to the heartiest soul. A breach in our mother-daughter relationship—perhaps caused by unhealed wounds, bitterness, or unfinished business—can make such a forever-task nearly unbearable.

Unfortunately, no one ever enjoys a perfect childhood. Every single one of us reaches adulthood with some wounds in need of healing, some resentments that need to be addressed. That reality is part of living in a fallen world. Yet some women deal with their wounds and resentments in an unhealthy way. They place themselves on the stand, confess their fault, accept all guilt, and pass sentence. The sentence? Responsibility for their mothers' happiness for the rest of their lives.

Others put their mothers on a mental witness stand, declare *her* guilty of causing their mortal wounds, dispense a life sentence, and then bang the gavel. They carry out her sentence by cutting her out of their lives, thereby trading one kind of unending responsibility for another. Sadly, some never stop to ask themselves whether all the relevant testimony has been considered before they declare the defendant guilty as charged. And the punishment rarely fits the "crime." How can adult daughters distinguish their rightful responsibility for their mothers?

MOTHER-BASHING: THAT EVER POPULAR GAME

Psychologists traditionally blame the mother when her children have problems. Sociologists blame her for the breakdown of the family when she works outside the home. Feminists blame her for keeping her children dependent when she chooses to work in the home, raising her children. Husbands blame her for depriving them by putting the children first. Children blame her for making mistakes and not giving them enough of what they need or want. When it so often seems like she's being set up as the designated scapegoat, it's a wonder any woman dares take on the task of motherhood.

Blaming may afford some temporary relief from uncomfortable emotions, but it can also prevent us from taking constructive steps toward an improved relationship. It seems easier to blame our mothers than to communicate with them. But blame usually provokes defensiveness. And a defensive response from the one who is blamed often causes an escalation of emotions on the part of the blamer. Before we know it, a vicious cycle has taken hold in which everyone suffers, including other family members who may be dragged, willy-nilly, into the fray.

What is the first step in taking responsibility for changing our mother-daughter relationships? Releasing ourselves and our mothers from condemnation and guilt. Doubtless, our mothers made mistakes in raising us. Just as doubtless, we were not always angelic in responding to our mothers. Regardless of the mistakes, no matter who made them, we can learn to take responsibility for our relationships now.

Rejecting the temptation to assign blame, however, doesn't mean that we can't speak the truth to our mothers. We don't suddenly decide to tell our mothers only what we think they want to hear. Those who are still hurting, or have resentments that must be addressed in order to clear the way for an improved relationship with their mothers, may need to take the risk and verbalize those wounds. We don't need to yell and scream or call our mothers names. But it is wise to calmly and lovingly tell the person involved what's eating us.

Telling the truth—however disturbing that truth may be—is one important way we can take responsibility for our relationships, and our lives. And if our mothers don't respond the way we had hoped, we at least have the comfort of knowing that we've been true to ourselves. In some cases, that knowledge is enough to salve the wounds and dispel the resentments.

A JOURNEY OF DISCOVERY

The aunts in Amy Tan's novel, *The Joy Luck Club*, were appalled by the thought that a woman might not be aware of the truths and hopes her own mother had possessed. They were horrified by the idea that a woman might be unable to recount her mother's personal story to future generations. They found it unthinkable for a woman not to take responsibility for *knowing* her mother.[1]

Our own culture doesn't place much emphasis on knowing our mothers. Perhaps it should. We need to understand our mothers, explore their stories, strive to understand their successes and their struggles. Not so that we can be forever responsible, but so that we may come that much closer to understanding ourselves.

If we refuse to recognize and understand the wounds of our mothers, the steps they have taken to salve those wounds, and the steps they may have taken to shield us from suffering those same wounds, we may be forever deprived of a profound level of self-knowledge. We must be willing to meet this challenge by finding out more about our mothers' lives, by becoming willing to listen to their suffering.

That's what inspired my friend, Gretta, to go back to explore her mother's roots. Gretta had lingering questions and unhealed wounds that were preventing her from making peace with her mother's recent death. Her mother, Inga, had never talked about her home, her family, or her early life. This adult daughter felt she needed to fill in some of the blanks in her knowledge of her mother and of her own roots.

Gretta decided to begin by visiting the small town where her mother grew up. She contacted her aunt and uncle who still lived there, and they invited her to visit them for a week. Elsie was delighted to help Gretta learn more about her sister, Inga. When Gretta arrived Elsie had an old scrapbook and mementos from their school years to show her. Since Hermann knew the people who lived in the home where Elsie and Inga grew up, he arranged to take his niece to see it.

The bus ride from the airport to the small town where her mother spent her first seventeen years gave Gretta time to ponder what it must have been like to grow up in that part of the country. Stepping off the bus was like walking into a whole new world for this young woman who had grown up in San Diego. After she returned home, Gretta told me about her experiences.

I hadn't seen my Aunt Elsie and Uncle Hermann since they visited my parents in San Diego more than twelve years ago, but I recognized my aunt as soon as I stepped off the bus because she looked like my mother. They were so happy to show me around the town, which looked like something out of the movies. The courthouse was in the middle of town and there were little shops on the street that circled the city park. The fruit trees were in bloom and that just made the quaint little town even more charming.

I was amazed by how emotional I felt just being there. My aunt pointed out the schools she and Mom had attended, reporting tidbits about Mom along the way. "Oh, she was popular, your mother! Did you know she was homecoming queen and that she was very much in love with the football team captain?"

Later, as we looked through Aunt Elsie's old high school yearbook, I was mesmerized by Mom's pictures. She came to life before my eyes. There she stood, a young, rather cocky looking teenager, with her arms freely slung around the boy who must have been the football hero, the first love of her life. I felt like I was walking on hallowed ground.

Aunt Elsie and I talked for hours. I had never heard most of what she told me. I felt I was getting to know my mother for the first time. Aunt Elsie shared both the painful and the joyful memories with me. Mom had never been able to do that. She never told me she had left home because of her father's strict disciplinary measures. I was angered by that, despite the fact that my grandparents have been dead a long time. Mom left home at seventeen to get away from her father's verbal accusations and put-downs.

My own father, a serviceman, became Mom's rescuer. She ran away with him. They were married in Utah on the way to California, and ended up spending the rest of their lives there. Mom had decided to put the past behind her when she married and moved so far away. She thought that would make her okay. But her wounds didn't just go away. They affected all of us for all of our lives. It would have been so helpful if I had understood Mom's suffering before she died. Learning about it helped to fill out my unfinished picture of her. But I'll always regret the fact that I waited until after Mom was gone before I got to know her.

As Gretta learned more about Inga's life, she understood why her mother had been adamantly opposed to Gretta dating at an early age. She had been attempting to protect Gretta from the difficult adjustments she had been forced to make as a result of her own early marriage. Unfortunately, this maternal ruling from on high had only intensified her daughter's rebellion. Inga had done her best as a parent to spare Gretta the pain she had endured as she was growing up.

Knowing about Inga's past gave Gretta insight into their mother-daughter dynamics. She could better understand some of the unspoken assumptions that had guided her mother's life. She managed to "settle accounts" with her Mom during that trip. Discovering her mother's personal history didn't make Gretta's pain go away, but she did appreciate the reasons behind some of her own struggles in growing up. These discoveries started the healing process.

THE IDEAL AND THE UNREAL

Mothers and daughters share *mutual* responsibility for their relationship as adults. The ideal would be for the two of them together to define their present relationship and then to decide what changes they would like to make. Sometimes, however, an interaction of that kind is simply not possible, either for practical or emotional reasons. Some of our mothers grew up in homes where discussing deeper emotional issues was forbidden. Those who are willing to learn to communicate will find the suggestions in this book easier to implement.

Some of you may be thinking, "You've got to be kidding! An act of Congress couldn't get my mother to talk freely about her feelings. She doesn't know she has them!" Don't give up hope. For every action there is an equal and opposite reaction—a fact which holds true within family dynamics as well as in physics. It is possible for you to make changes in your attitude and behavior that will significantly affect your mother-daughter relationship, whether or not you're able to enlist your mother's cooperation.

What is the first move you can make toward that end? Take responsibility for yourself now, in the present. That means taking responsibility for your feelings and your behavior, regardless of what events from your past may have prompted them.

The second move you can make is equally important. Place the responsibility for your mother's feelings and actions where it belongs—with *her.* You don't have the power to "make" your mother feel hurt, or angry, or left out, anymore than you have the power to "make" her feel happy or empowered. Only she has that ability. You are responsible for treating your mother with courtesy and love. You are not responsible for her reaction to the firm but loving statements you make or changes you may choose to set into motion in your relationship. You can offer to help her talk through her reactions if you like, but you are *not* responsible for them—a crucial distinction.

Often, the problems adult women have with their mothers are related to the violation of personal boundaries. Mothers sometimes find it difficult to exchange the relationship they had with young offspring—a relationship in which few bound-aries exist—for the sort of relationship necessary to the health and well-being of young people and adults. When mothers continue to relate to their adult children in much the same manner as in childhood, those daughters are bound to feel demeaned and intruded upon. We obviously no longer need our mothers to remind us to wash our hands before dinner or to help us bathe.

But subtler forms of boundary violations may not be so obvious, even though they may be just as uncomfortable—and just as detrimental to intimacy between us. When a woman feels devalued, dominated, used, and controlled by her mother, it's extremely difficult for her to discover who she is in her own right. And the price of that violation, or that lack of individuality, is an absence of true intimacy.

Many families view a lack of appropriate boundaries as intimacy, but it's only an inappropriate counterfeit. True inti-macy is impossible between two people who aren't sure where one begins and the other leaves off. And we can only be sure of that when we have boundaries that delineate both our emotional and physical territory from that of another—even our mothers.

WHAT IS A BOUNDARY?

The word "boundaries" is bandied about a lot these days, but most people only have a very sketchy notion of what it really means. A boundary is simply a border that defines our personal territory, which may encompass actual physical space or an emotional zone.

Psychotherapists Nancy Wasserman Cocola and Arlene Modica Matthews explain the notion of boundaries this way: "Boundaries are delicate places of proximity. When people cross them carelessly, they are potential friction zones. When they are approached properly, as when citizens of one country present passports and visas at various checkpoints so they may visit another country for a limited duration, there is little cause for border skirmishes."[2] Because they are more subjective and intangible, emotional boundaries may be a little more difficult to define than the borders of a country, but practice can teach us to recognize those as well.

A family learns numerous ways of defining boundaries for its members. Physical boundaries are maintained by closing bedroom and bathroom doors and by having separate beds for family members. Knocking at a door before entering is a form of presenting one's passport and visa. By not granting permission to enter, the occupant of that space declares that your visa is not approved at that particular moment. If the knocker ignores the refusal and barges in anyway, a border skirmish is likely to follow. That skirmish will probably be an emotional one rather than a physical one but, in the long run, it can be just as deadly to a relationship.

Emotional boundaries are maintained by respecting each member's spoken and unspoken messages regarding their personal "comfort zones." Children should be given the right to refuse to be touched or hugged when it doesn't feel comfortable or "safe." Children should be given the right to privacy in the bathroom and their bedroom that's appropriate for their age and physical needs. Older children should have the assurance that their belongings will not be disturbed by parents or siblings in their absence.

A lack of respect for boundaries within the family results in constant—although often unconscious—vigilance. Anxiety runs high, even when family members can't quite explain why. In the case of pervasive neglect of individual boundaries, anxiety may be such a constant for family members that they may not be consciously aware of it. The anxiety has become too thoroughly woven into the fabric of their lives to be discernable as a single thread.

As adult women we need our mothers to interact with us the same way they would any adult. Just being the mother doesn't give anyone license to comment on housekeeping, hair, clothes, or child-rearing techniques without a specific invitation to do so.

If you find yourself grinding your teeth when you're in your mother's presence, it's probably safe to assume the presence of some unresolved boundary issues. Here are some brief guidelines to help you gauge whether the boundaries you maintain between you and the rest of the world are healthy or perhaps in need of clearer delineation.[3]

- Are you aware of your own preferences and do you freely act upon them?
- Do you trust your own intuition?
- Do you engage in self-enhancing projects?
- Are you able to calmly counter another's attempt to manipulate you?
- Do you negotiate differences and act out of agreement rather than out of a desire to avoid rocking the boat?
- Do you make your own choices?
- Are you living the life you want to live as opposed to living someone else's dream?
- Do you protect your privacy without feeling you need to lie or make excuses in order to do so?
- Can you tell when you're happy or unhappy?
- Do you lovingly hold others accountable for their actions rather than swallowing your hurt or discomfort?

Are some of these qualities missing from your mother-daughter relationship? You can take responsibility, beginning right now, for finding ways to change. One way to begin changing immediately is by making plans to gently thwart unhealthy recurring patterns between you and your mother.

A FRESH PERSPECTIVE

Everybody in the family agreed that Katelyn's mom, Catherine, was a sweet and compassionate busybody. But Katelyn found it increasingly difficult to grin and bear it when her mother dropped by unannounced "just to check in." With three children under the age of five, the first thought that usually came into Katelyn's mind when she saw her mother's familiar car pulling into the driveway was, "Why me?" And some variation on the theme, "Why didn't I run the vacuum this morning?" Her second thought was always, "Why can't she ever call first?" Many times Katelyn wanted nothing more than a trap door installed in her front porch.

After a particularly hectic visit, Katelyn had finally had enough. She decided that she must take some sort of action soon. If not, she would eventually do or say something that would seriously damage her relationship with her mother.

Katelyn sat down at her kitchen table with a tablet of paper that night and brainstormed. The next time Catherine turned up on Katelyn's doorstep she was ready for her. Instead of sitting down with her mother at the kitchen table and drinking coffee—as visions of unwashed clothing danced in her head—she enlisted her mother's aid with the children so that she could "just get a few things done" while help was available.

Katelyn continued to chat pleasantly while she worked but treated her mother like a comrade-at-arms rather than a visiting potentate. When Catherine remarked about the fact that Katelyn never seemed to find the time to polish the copper bottoms of her pots and pans, she smiled sweetly and told her mother where the copper polish was as she continued sorting laundry and wiping runny noses.

The next time Catherine dropped by Katelyn exclaimed, "How wonderful! The kids have been telling me that they wish we could get out to the park more, but it's so hard for one adult to take three small children to the park. With you along, it'll be easy." She promptly put sweaters on all three children and everyone, including Grandma, piled into the car and headed for the park. Katelyn spent the time chatting amiably with her mom while they took turns running after children who had ventured too far from the play area.

Katelyn had decided ahead of time that her mother could have two possible reactions to this new approach to her visits. Catherine might get tired of being "drafted" to help and would stop dropping by unannounced. Or Grandma would enjoy making herself useful and Katelyn would be free to relax and enjoy her visits without feeling that her mother was imposing on her and disrupting her routine. Because she felt at the end of her tether when she finally adopted her plan, Katelyn didn't really care which reaction she got. She just knew she needed a change.

I talked with Katelyn the other day and she's happy to report that her mother loves feeling useful. In fact, Katelyn called me, laughing, because her mom—this woman who was so opposed to calling ahead—has begun to call her once a week to ask, "How can I be the most help this week? What would be the best day for me to drop by?"

Katelyn confided to me, "Now I can't figure out why I agonized over making this change. It's the best thing that's happened to me and my mom since I moved away from home. She's rapidly becoming my best friend. And I *never* thought that could happen!"

Sometimes the change that's necessary in order to protect a boundary is nothing more than a change in our perspective. Naturally, not every plan for change will turn out as neatly as Katelyn's. But approaching the change calmly, with a plan that's aimed at increasing our comfort without making an enemy of our mothers, will probably net healthy results. And deep down, most mothers want what's best for their daughters. We simply need to define, first for ourselves and then for our mothers, what that is.

Exercises

1. List on a piece of paper all the things about your relationship for which you blame your mother. Write down all the things for which you blame yourself. Now hold an imaginary trial, at which you are the prosecutor and defender of each list. Ask if all the evidence is in. Let yourself be the jury and see if you can give a fair and objective verdict.

2. Discuss your list with your mother—either in your imagination or in real life. Allow her to make a rebuttal to the list of wrongs if she desires.

3. Are you guilty of mother-bashing? How have you engaged in such words or behavior and how has it impacted her?

4. What do you know about your mother's past? Can you call to mind important details of her early history? What are some questions about her life that you would like to ask her?

5. Check yourself out on the list of boundary guidelines. Where do you feel strong or weak? How are you and your mother working out appropriate boundaries as adults? If you're not satisfied with your boundaries, what would you like to do to improve them?

FOUR

~~~~~~~~~~~

Bonding, Abandonment, Connection, and Love

"**I**T'S A GIRL!" An elated mother may hear that pronounce-
ment from the doctor and immediately think, "Like
mother, like daughter!" Face-to-face for the first time, close
together with baby cradled in mother's arms, all their senses
are at work helping them get acquainted. The soft contact of
skin on skin makes an indelible impression. Perhaps no bond
is closer.

It may not always be love at first sight, but bonding some-
what resembles the "falling in love" process. Mother and
daughter come together in an intimate encounter. Baby com-
municates with coos, relaxing in the comfort of her mother's
arms, smiling in response to her mother's nurturing voice.
Mother responds, in turn, with similar loving sounds. Totally
engrossed in each other's world, they give themselves to each
other absolutely, holding nothing back.

A mother must make her baby's welfare a primary focus simply because an infant is so utterly helpless. Early bonding provides the experience of unconditional love. Faithful maternal care is the firm foundation upon which a baby's trust is built.

Psychoanalyst D.W. Winnecott, describes the bonding between mother and baby this way: "At this very early state, it is not logical to think of an individual.... If you set out to describe a baby, you will find that you are describing a baby and someone. A baby cannot exist alone, but is essentially part of a relationship."[1] Two separate entities reside within a single body during the pregnancy. Now the two bodies share in a single relationship.

Mother and daughter for life! Mother and daughter for better or worse! Mother and daughter for richer or poorer! Mother and daughter in sickness and in health! Mother and daughter until death! A mother commits herself unconditionally to her totally dependent baby, just as the helpless infant entrusts herself totally to her all-powerful mother. The bonding experience brings out a deep sense of wonder, a previously unknown sense of responsibility for a woman, even if she's already shouldered immense responsibilities in other areas of her life.

Many cultures hold among their basic tenets the assumption that a mother's love should be unconditional. What an amazing idea that one human could love another *unconditionally!* Yet putting the needs of a helpless infant ahead of one's own needs and desires can be extremely difficult, day after day after day. Mothers must reach deep within themselves—and ultimately to the grace of God—to find the needed resources. Unfortunately, human love often fails. The intensity of the baby's total dependency, coupled with the fact that a mother must give much more to her baby than she receives, sometimes land on a mother's shoulders with crushing force.

Successful bonding doesn't depend only on the mother, however. The baby has her part in the bonding process, as well. Babies are incapable of thinking to themselves, "Well, just because Mom didn't come when I cried this time doesn't mean she's not a good person. She came the last three times I cried." When a baby's needs are not being met at the moment, she perceives her mother as "all bad" and responds accordingly. When her needs are being satisfied, she perceives mother as "all good" and acceptable.

The truth is, all mothers will inevitably fail their children. Circumstances in a mother's life will eventually interfere with her ability to meet her baby's every need. Even though mothers intuitively know they can't do the job perfectly, many find it tremendously difficult to openly admit or accept that fact. That's when the concept of being a "good-enough" mother can be a life saver.

Adequate bonding is possible without perfect mothering. A mother doesn't have to spend every waking moment of her life with her baby, meeting the darling's every need. In fact, admitting her limitations gives a mother the ability to accept them without being devastated. And, of course, a mother who is accepting of herself and her own limits will tend to be a calmer, happier, more confident mother. She needs to learn to accept support from others during the less-than-blissful times in her child's life. She needs to replenish herself with friends and activities separate from her baby so that, in the long run, she has more to give her baby.

Some adult daughters tend to heap sweeping praise even upon mothers who undoubtedly made many mistakes over the years. "My mother was always there for me." "I knew I could count on her." "She never gave up on me." "I never doubted her love." Such women have experienced unconditional love from their mothers. Because these women gained the precious ability to trust early in life, they usually retain a similar capacity as adults.

Women can often recall some of their childhood lessons about unconditional love. Carolyn remembers having an argument with her mother when she was eight years old. The little girl ran to her room and slammed the door behind her. She took out her diary and began to write. Carolyn's furious feelings spilled out into some nasty words. But as she cooled down, she shifted to a different tone and wrote this on the last page, "Mom, even when we're mad at each other, I know you will still love me." In that moment, she was aware of her mother's unconditional love, a love that could never be taken away.

Carolyn had learned the difficult lesson that anger was not necessarily the end of love—her own love or her mother's. That knowledge had a profound impact on her adult life. What a wonderful gift for those of us who have the good fortune to learn that lesson at our mother's knee.

WHEN THE SUPER-GLUE OF LOVE FAILS

This crucial bonding process can be hampered by a mother's preconceived notions and unrealistic expectations either about herself or the baby. From the very beginning, Gini doubted her ability to bond with her baby. Mothering seemed such an awesome task to this twenty-one-year-old. Acutely aware of how fragile her baby seemed, Gini worried that this tiny little life could be snuffed out in a second if she was not able to provide proper care. The baby's helplessness and dependency triggered her fears of inadequacy. Gini became paralyzed by this fear that she would be a negligent mother. Her fears prevented healthy bonding.

Another woman, Dawn, found that her own expectations for what her daughter would be like kept her from responding positively. Her red, squinty-faced, bald, baby girl was nothing like she had imagined. This little stranger would take some getting used to. Gradually Dawn opened her heart to her baby and they managed to bond despite their rough start.

Giving birth doesn't automatically cause a mother to bond with her baby. Significant changes and adjustments are required of a mother in the first few weeks after birth. She ends her pregnancy and immediately undergoes a dramatic change in her lifestyle—whether the baby is her first or her tenth. She must adapt to the new baby, take on or readjust her role as mother, accept the baby, let go of false expectations, face her fears of inadequacy, make room for Daddy, and learn to cope with the enormous demands the baby makes on her time and energy.

All of these demands clamor for the mother's attention at the same time her own body is going through countless physical and hormonal changes! It's as if we're asking a new mother to change into superwoman without benefit of a telephone booth. No wonder so many women experience the blues shortly after the birth of a child.

Of course, this whole scenario assumes the absence of unusual difficulties. Imagine having to care for twins or triplets! What if the baby is born prematurely and needs to remain in the hospital for a few more weeks? What if the newborn infant turns out to have a serious physical deformity or health problem? What if the baby has Down's syndrome or cerebral palsy or any of a whole host of other genetic abnormalities? What if the mother is already in her late forties and having to unhook from her dreams of an empty nest? What if the mother is alone and destitute?

Even in ideal circumstances, few women are aware of how challenging this transition can be. The losses inherent in adding a new participant in one's life must be acknowledged and grieved before the gains can be claimed and appreciated. Investigating the dynamics of your early bonding years can help you to understand your current ability to bond with your mother as well as with others in your life.

In an effort to make up for early deprivation, daughters who failed to bond properly with their mothers often make unreasonable demands on friends, partners, or children. Because of the neglect they suffered during childhood, these women may also strike out in anger whenever they feel others have neglected their needs in the present.

For others, anger may not be an occasional reaction. This very effective tool in keeping people at arm's length may become more pervasive. People who typically use anger as a defense mechanism believe, somewhere deep within, that they'll be hurt again if they allow themselves to be vulnerable.

Self-sufficiency is another way to make sure no one will get too close. Those who rely primarily on themselves avoid the necessity of leaning on someone else who may fail them. And, eventually, everyone will, because they are only human. But detachment born of self-sufficiency sadly exiles these people to an island of loneliness.

Other women connect in desperate, possessive ways as a compensation for insufficient bonding. They almost seek to engulf another person in order to fill the needy chasm created by their early deprivation. Since no one likes feeling overwhelmed by another's neediness, husbands and/or children of these women often protect themselves by adopting distancing techniques. This, in turn, intensifies an already overwhelming sense of abandonment for such women.

The few people who seem willing to even try to meet the needs of someone who has suffered childhood deprivation are often motivated by the need to be needed. Such a person is often referred to as a "rescuer." His or her own neediness tends to spawn obsessive and/or co-dependent relationships.

These are just a few examples of the endless ways in which many of us learn to cope with the pain resulting from faulty bonding in early childhood. These coping methods act a lot like shadow boxing. They never deal with the *source* of our pain. Rather, we often wear down by engaging in useless dodging and fancy footwork in an effort to escape the blows we believe originate from outside ourselves.

Nothing any of us can do will ever rectify or erase the events of the past. But we can take responsibility for claiming our healing in the present. Most of us find it much easier to recognize and heal that lingering pain once we are consciously aware of its origin. This chapter is designed to help you become more conscious of the source of your pain so that you can face it head on and receive God's healing touch.

JUST LIKE ME

Bonding with a daughter is different from bonding with a son for a number of reasons. A mother automatically identifies her daughter as someone *similar* to her while she sees her son as one who is *different* from her. Most women connect more easily with a daughter than with a son, although some may have more difficulty connecting with the same sex child. Generally, a mother feels more comfortable and natural with one who is like her.

Here are some women's descriptions of their initial reactions to the announcement, "It's a girl!" Carol says that she cringed inside when she heard the announcement because she had wanted a boy! Disturbed by her immediate reaction, she wondered why she would have preferred a boy. Upon reflection Carol realized that she was worried that a daughter might become so close to her husband that it would pose a threat to her marriage. She knew that she had competed with her girlfriends over boys and was afraid she might have to compete with a daughter for her husband's attention.

For Evelyn, coming home from the hospital was a joyful occasion. She felt grateful that her in-laws were going to be there for a few days to lend support. Her joy was short-lived, however. Evelyn quickly sensed that her in-laws were disappointed that the baby wasn't a boy. After they left she experienced feelings of loneliness and sadness. Evelyn felt that she had failed her husband and his family by not giving them a son. And, realizing that her daughter was destined to grow up in a family that preferred boys, she feared for her daughter's future.

Karen was thrilled to have a baby girl. In fact, she became so focused on the mother-daughter duo that she failed to welcome her husband into the intimate circle. Something seemed almost sacred about nursing her daughter. The new mother found herself wondering whether she should allow her husband to touch her breasts. Karen was surprised by this desire to keep him out of their special relationship. She wanted her baby all to herself.

These mothers were all grappling with gender-related issues. Whether a baby is a boy or a girl makes a difference to everyone within a family. What's more, family attitudes about a child's gender help to determine that child's sense of self. It is inevitably communicated to a child, in one way or another, when a family member wants, or wanted, a child of the opposite sex, even when that preference is supposedly a secret.

Not only is gender a factor in bonding, it's a factor in the separation process as well. Nancy Chodorow, author of *The Reproduction of Mothering*,[2] suggests that a girl's identity comes from connection and identification with her mother, while a son's identity comes through separating from his mother and identifying with his father. Chodorow believes that a daughter's sense of self is deeply rooted in the experience of her earliest relationship with her mother.

Psychologist, Robin Skynner, pictures the gender identification process like a river flowing between two banks.[3] Mother and children stand on one side while father stands on the opposite bank. When appropriate identification occurs, the daughter and mother remain together on the same bank of the river while a boy must break away from mother and forge the river in order to identify with his father. In order to identify as a male, a son must make this dramatic break, which he often does by shunning anything that smacks of femaleness. Separating from his mother, who is generally his first love object, can be an emotional ordeal.

The mother, in anticipation of this separation, may guard against becoming overly connected with her son in order to protect herself from the pain of letting him go. If she holds on too tightly, he may have difficulty perceiving himself as a male. Friends may call this child "a mama's boy" unless he musters the courage to make this emotional break and identify with his father or some other male role model. Chodorow has noted that this may be one reason males tend to resist being dependent on women.

Establishing an identity is an entirely different experience for the female child. A daughter doesn't need to break the bonds with her mother in order to establish herself as a female. She bonds with one who is like her and she wholeheartedly accepts her mother's imprint. She recognizes that her father is different from her, but she doesn't have to separate from him or negate anything that suggests maleness in order to find her identity.

A girl's separation from her mother is more gradual and may come a bit later than it does for a boy child. Waiting longer, however, may make it more difficult for a daughter to establish independence and separate herself from her mother. Girls in their teens sometimes attempt to separate with such a vengeance for this very reason, although their efforts aren't always as successful as all the fireworks might indicate. And many young women never even attempt to separate. Girls in our society tend to be rewarded for connecting; males are rewarded for separating. These gender-related tendencies seem to continue throughout life.

THE RHYTHMIC EBB AND FLOW

Connection and separation are important aspects of the mother/baby relationship. The birthing ordeal is merely the first of many separation crises for mother and child. After birth, although a blanket, crib, or nursery wall creates a physical separation, mother and baby can be connected emotionally in a person-to-person interaction that was impossible when they occupied one body.

This cycle of connection and separation continues throughout the growth of the child. Have you ever watched a five-month-old child who has just learned to crawl away from mother? She streaks across the room, stops, then suddenly realizes she's separated from her mother, panics, and comes scrambling back. It's humorous to watch the baby discover that her newfound freedom has produced too much distance as she scrambles back for reassurance of that necessary connection with her mother.

We can see this picture of mother-daughter relationships reenacted again and again throughout life. As a daughter gains increasing independence, her freedom provides the physical and emotional distance she seeks. But that distance may feel too scary at times. When it does, the daughter comes streaking back for reassurance. This rhythmic cycle of separation and connection is part of God's plan for children.

A daughter who has repeatedly and successfully connected, separated, and reconnected, has learned that physical and emotional separation doesn't mean a loss of love. She's learned that independence can be achieved without sacrificing a healthy interdependence. Daughters who learn that they can count on their mothers to be there when they come streaking back for reassurance will be able to establish a healthy interdependence in all or most of their later relationships.

In the case of a mother and her newborn, as in all of life,

separation is a necessary step toward genuine intimacy. I believe that a person can't achieve a healthy separation until she's sufficiently connected, and that she can't connect with genuine intimacy unless she's sufficiently separate. Keeping a balance between these two aspects of our relationships isn't just important; it's essential.

When a daughter is separated from her mother before adequate bonding is achieved, serious difficulties can arise. If a child has been neglected, abandoned, or separated from her mother in her first year of life, the disruption can have long-term ramifications. Judith Viorst in her book, *Necessary Losses*, makes this statement about separation:

> If our mother leaves us—when we are too young, too unprepared, too scared, too helpless—the cost of this leaving, the cost of this loss, the cost of this separation may be too high.... Unless we are ready to separate—unless we are ready to leave her and be left—anything is better than separation.... We can endure anything but abandonment... the pain is unimaginable. The healing is hard and slow. The damage, although not fatal, may be permanent.[4]

Developmental psychologists generally agree. Disruption in the bonding process has long-lasting effects. While abandonment during the early years of life may not be fatal, it often dents a person's ability to eventually bond and be intimate with others. We take the "love bond" with our mother into ourselves as a foundation upon which we can then build love for ourselves and others. Abandonment at this early stage leaves us with a shaky foundation. If we're starved for love—yet see ourselves as unloveable at some level—we become convinced that we will never find what we so desperately need.

Susan remembers being terrified as a little girl that her mother would leave her in a large department store. Even at the age of twelve, Susan was afraid to stay overnight with relatives because she couldn't bear to be separated from her mother. "I thought she was trying to get rid of me! I couldn't let her out of my sight. I remember playing sad songs on the piano, belting out the words with sobs, 'You're breaking my heart 'cause you're leaving, you've fallen for somebody new. It isn't too easy believing, you'd leave after all we've been through.'"

Susan's separation anxiety became even more pronounced when she began dating. She clung to her boyfriends, sure they would eventually jilt her for somebody else. After Susan married, she found it difficult to trust her husband, Sam. Although this young woman couldn't admit it to him or to herself, this newlywed felt sure that her husband would fall in love with another woman and abandon her. Because she clung to him so tightly, Sam felt suffocated and found himself wanting to push her away.

One day Sam admitted that he was attracted to another woman. Her worst nightmare had come to life! This revelation caused a memory to surface in her mind. Susan remembered hanging on to her mother when she was afraid to spend the night with a friend. She began to search her past, seeking some reason for her fearful approach to life. Where had these feelings of abandonment originated? Could it be that she had contributed in some strange way to what was happening to her marriage?

In her search for more information, Susan found an important clue in her own baby book. Here are the words her mother wrote when Susan was just eleven months old:

Entry dated 4/15/45: I sent you to stay with your Aunt Gracie and Uncle Harry for a few months while I am getting ready to have my next baby. It was hard to wake up this morning to an empty crib because I loved hearing your sweet little voice cooing to me in the mornings. I miss you so much!

Entry dated 6/15/45: You have made Mommy feel very sad today. Aunt Gracie brought you home and when she said goodbye to you, you cried after her, "Ma! Ma!" You wouldn't come to me and you cried and cried all night.

Here was what Susan had been searching to find. From her eleven-month-old perspective, she had been abandoned by her mother. What an immense violation of trust for a little one to endure! Granted, Susan had been able to form an attachment to her aunt during those two crucial months of her life. But she actually ended up experiencing a second abandonment when she was wrenched from the security of that bond as well. As a result, the message, "Don't trust, because those you love will leave you" was etched deep in her unconscious.

Broken trust in this early developmental stage leaves a person on rocky ground when it comes to trusting others in life. As a consequence, Susan struggled with a fear of abandonment even as an adult. Her mother and aunt had intended no malice; in fact, they were loving, supportive, nurturing women. Yet because of their ignorance, Susan had to live with self-doubts and insecurity about her worthiness to be loved. She constantly feared that she would be abandoned without warning.

Susan put it this way: "Even though I can understand it intellectually and have experienced a consistent, unconditional love from my mother in my adult life, I still feel uneasy and insecure about my worth. I often fight the fear that my husband or friends will leave me. Now that I know about the roots of my fears I'm able to talk freely to my mom and my husband about them and that's been very helpful in my effort to put them into perspective."

Susan and her husband were able to work through his attraction to the other woman as they began to understand more about her childhood trauma. In the process, Sam expressed his difficulty with his wife's clinging behavior and learned ways to assure her of his love and commitment. And Susan learned to verbalize when she was feeling particularly fearful. She also began to build lasting relationships with Christian friends who could love her faithfully and unconditionally. She still feels fear in the pit of her stomach at times, but now she has an awareness of where that fear originates and can deal with it forthrightly.

Important seeds are planted, for good or ill, in our earliest relationship, which is usually with our mothers. Bonding, connection, unconditional love, separation, and autonomy are aspects of this early relationship that continue to affect us throughout our lives. You may find it helpful to gain some insight into what sort of bond existed between you and your mother. You may glean some important clues about recurring themes in your current relationships. Take time to do the following exercises and write about your own bonding experience.

You may want to read your baby book and ask questions of your mother, father, siblings, grandparents, aunts, and uncles about your early childhood. Find out what was happening in the family and in the world during the time of your birth that may have affected your mother's ability to bond with you in "good enough" ways.

How might you have contributed to the process? Ask how others responded to you. Did you have tantrums? Were you friendly? Did you withdraw? Asking such questions will help you to understand your bonding experience with your mother. Perhaps you bonded with a surrogate—a housekeeper, babysitter, grandparent, aunt, etc. You may want to place some of your focus on that person as well.

If you have the opportunity, share some of these ideas and feelings with your mother. Get her perspective on what she experienced during these early bonding years. It will help you fill in the details and get an idea of what was happening for her at the time of your birth and how that influenced you. You have everything to gain and nothing to lose.

Exercises

1. Take some time to relax and let yourself think back to the time of your birth. What did your mother look like, where was she living, and what was she doing?

2. What special circumstances surrounded your mother's pregnancy that may have contributed to her feelings about your birth? (These might include a death in the family, financial concerns, career decisions, whether you were a long awaited child or a surprise, and so forth.)

3. Think about your family constellation when you were born. Was the marital relationship intact, stable, happy, strained? Were there other siblings in the family at the time of your birth? What were their ages and gender? What difference did it make to them and to you that you were born a girl?

4. How were you received into your family? Were there important extended family members and/or friends that took an interest in your birth? Did your mother have a support system when she was worn out or needed a breather?

5. Did a good bonding occur between you and your mother? Why or why not? How do you think this impacts you today? What are your feelings about it?

6. How do you tend to respond to your current relationships when it comes to connection and separation? Can you see any patterns that may be the result of your own early bonding experience?

FIVE

Mother, Do You Like Who I Am?

Twenty-seven-year-old Brenda was engaged in a heated argument with her mother over the way she dressed. Brenda tended to dress very simply, wearing tailored suits to work and jeans and tee shirts at home. Leaning toward ruffles and lace herself, her mother expressed the opinion that her daughter's image would benefit if she wore more "feminine" clothing. As the disagreement continued, Brenda's mother became agitated and abruptly left.

Later on, Brenda began feeling bad about the altercation. Realizing that their differences were superficial, she went to her mother to patch things up. Despite their differences, she wanted her mother to know that she loved her. It took courage for Brenda to take that step. Her family did not freely express feelings of affection to one another. Sadly, the mother was unable to receive her daughter's message of love. She turned away with the chilling comment, "Sometimes I wonder if you know what love is!"

Instead of accepting and forgiving, Brenda's mother chose to cling to her anger—all because her daughter wasn't what she wanted her to be. Her mental monologue may have gone something like this: "If you loved me, you'd do what I want you to do. Obviously you don't love me. I have the right not to accept or forgive you until you prove you love me by dressing to please me." In other words, Brenda had to give up her self in order to be loved by her mother. That was a sacrifice too great to make.

Fortunately, Brenda had learned as an adult that she didn't need to please her mother at every turn. She continued to demonstrate her love for her mother while still dressing according to her own tastes. Since her mother seemed unable to accept Brenda's taste in clothes, the daughter sweetly and tactfully changed the subject whenever it came up after that. Usually, it only took a query like, "What do you think of the food, Mother?" or "Did you hear that cousin Jean is going to have *six* bridesmaids at her wedding?" Some such innocuous distraction usually accomplished her goal. Sometimes the best policy is simply to agree to disagree, even when that approach can only be voiced within our own minds.

EXPECTATIONS: TWO SIZES TOO BIG

Most mothers don't expect their daughters to be carbon copies of themselves. Even so, the desire to be accepted by our mothers remains a powerful, inner urge for most daughters. Even as adults, many of us continue to work hard for their approval. We try to please them; we seek their advice. Unfortunately, in our eagerness to please our mothers, we sometimes fail to develop qualities that are of particular importance to us.

Mothers anticipate that their sons will differ, but most mothers assume that their daughters will be like them, at least to some extent. Such an expectation can create significant problems. Although mother and daughter are biologically similar and pass through parallel developmental stages, they each experience the world differently. We all possess unique personalities and temperaments. Very early, many daughters begin to wonder whether they are acceptable in their own right—or only when they assume the image they believe their mothers project onto them.

Every mother will naturally cling to dreams for her daughters. To expect otherwise would be unrealistic. But when daughters feel pressured to fulfill those dreams instead of following their own, trouble begins to brew. On the other hand, when mothers consciously set aside their own personal expectations and encourage their daughters to become unique selves, the little flower can begin to blossom.

Diana laughed as she described the day she came face-to-face with her own unrealistic expectations. This particular mother-daughter interaction provides a very tangible illustration of this concept of oversized expectations:

"My mother and I went shopping for a coat for my daughter, Joy, who was three years old at the time. We had looked in a zillion stores. And then we saw it! A gorgeous, fabulous, golden, velvet coat! It was just perfect and we both fell in love with it. The price was right and we couldn't wait to get home to see how Joy looked in it.

"We were so excited as we called her into the room and bundled her up in her new little coat. But, to our surprise, it was much too big for her and she literally fell over backwards with the weight of that coat on her little shoulders. It was the funniest thing I have ever seen. She didn't get hurt or anything, but I can still remember how she looked, stiff as a board, like the little, steadfast tin soldier, when she fell straight back to the floor."

This comical scene is inelibly imprinted on Diana's memory. It provides her with a picture of how often she loads things onto her daughter's shoulders before her daughter is ready. And Diana admits that she does the same thing to herself. Now, when she catches herself in the act of placing or receiving unrealistic expectations, Diana recalls the vivid image of Joy falling flat on her back. That mental photograph gives her the courage to go over, put her arm around Joy, and relieve her daughter of a load that's two sizes too big.

Some mothers actually hope their daughters *won't* turn out like them. They pray that their daughters will find life more fulfilling or more challenging than they did. Or that they'll find more peace and happiness. Believe it or not, even those expectations can become stumbling blocks to a daughter. Such fearful messages—however subtly conveyed—can leave a daughter with a nagging feeling that perhaps she is not finding *enough* fulfillment or challenge or peace or happiness. Any expectation that hinders our efforts to follow our own God-ordained paths can cause us trouble.

Whether we believe that our mothers wanted us to be too much like them or very different, we need to make a conscious effort to identify verbalized messages or unspoken expectations. What strong message does a growing daughter need to hear again and again? *Acceptance.* The invitation simply to *be*, without shame or apology. In the words of a song written by the children's television personality, Mr. Rogers, this message affirms:

> I like you as you are,
>   exactly and precisely.
> I think you turned out nicely
>   and I like you as you are.

Acceptance means embracing a person just as she is. Naturally, it's nearly impossible for any human being to be absolutely accepting of another person at all times. God is the only person able to pull off that feat. And in my experience, the people who seem to be the most accepting of others are the ones who are most conscious of God's acceptance of them. "Beloved, let us love one another; because love is from God; everyone who loves is born of God and knows God. Whoever does not love does not know God; for God is love" (1 Jn 4:7-8).

Many of us never feel unconditionally accepted by our very human mothers. Growing up without this firm foundation makes it exceedingly difficult to develop healthy self-esteem. The message that we are unacceptable as we are —whether declared loudly or silently—continues to echo in our minds. The implication follows that we must become something or someone else if we're ever going to be acceptable. That kind of rejection from the most important person in our young lives produces a deep feeling of shame. We're ashamed of our choices, our impulses—of who we are.

HERE COMES THE JUDGE!

Some of us never stop fearing disapproval. Karley's mother bombards her with questions every time she visits. She gets the distinct impression that her mother doesn't approve of the way she's managing her life. Gladys preaches her ten-thousandth sermon about the health hazards of smoking, gives her daughter an article about lung cancer, and scolds her for not having the moral strength to quit—all despite the fact that Karley is fifty years old! Gladys can't give up telling her daughter what to do despite the way it drives them apart. Because her visits only begin negative encounters where there are no winners, only losers, Karley visits more and more infrequently.

Kim's problem is the reverse. She's disappointed with her

mother. "I'm ashamed to have my friends see her in her pink glow blouse and tight jeans. She's living a lifestyle that I don't approve of and cannot accept." Recently, when I visited Kim's mother, she sadly remarked, "Kim's ashamed of me! I'm proud of her, but she's not proud of me. That makes *me* feel ashamed. I'm not good enough for her." Betty feels that Kim questions not only her behavior but her worth as a human being. The situation is very sad for both of them.

Do you ever play the blame/shame game? "See what happens when you don't listen to me?!" "You weren't there for me when I needed you, so don't expect me to call you next time!" Such attacks pierce to our innermost core. Like Kim's mother, we sometimes feel deeply shamed when an accusing finger is pointed in our direction.

In *Facing Shame: Families in Recovery*, Merle Fossum and Marilyn Mason note that shame is much more than loss of face or embarrassment:

> Shame is an inner sense of being completely diminished or insufficient as a person. It is the self judging the self. A moment of shame may be humiliation so painful or an indignity so profound that one feels one has been robbed of her or his dignity or exposed as basically inadequate, bad, or worthy of rejection. A pervasive sense of shame is the ongoing premise that one is fundamentally bad, inadequate, defective, unworthy, or not fully valid as a human being.[1]

Guilt is an appropriate response to misbehavior. When we break our code of ethics, we feel bad. We are sorry for the offense and search for ways to mend our relationships. In contrast, shame is a painful feeling that causes us to condemn our very selves. That condemnation can lead to hopelessness and a feeling of powerlessness. We can become embroiled in a vicious cycle of trying to please, while secretly believing we'll never be good enough. Self-doubts haunt us through those internalized "I can't" messages that lead to more failure, shame, and self-doubt.

In shame-bound relationships the shame and despair we feel about ourselves prevents us from taking positive, responsible action within the relationship.[2] Loranna was troubled by a number of "little things" when she began therapy. Her doctor had told her that she was just a bored housewife. His prescription: "Go out and get a job." But Loranna sensed that there was more to it than that. Having felt generally depressed and weepy of late, she was particularly concerned because she couldn't seem to look at herself in a mirror without bursting into tears.

As therapy progressed Loranna began to get in touch with a core of shame within her. Her mother, an unforgiving taskmaster, had criticized her constantly and harshly when she was a child. Lee criticized the way her daughter looked, the way she walked, the way she related to her friends. Loranna spent many therapy sessions processing her grief and shame. Eventually, she decided to confront her mother about the way she had been treated.

Screwing up her courage, Loranna arranged to meet her mother at a friend's beach house one weekend. What transpired was far beyond anything she could have asked or imagined. Loranna first expressed her appreciation for some of the good things her mother had done for her when she was growing up. Then she carefully and lovingly told Lee about some of the work she had been doing in therapy. She talked about the shame she felt and some of the reasons for that shame.

As she talked Lee began to weep. Seeing her mother's tears made Loranna falter for just a moment. She almost decided that her own peace of mind and desire for a closer relationship weren't worth the hurt she must be causing her mother by her words. But then Loranna remembered what I had told her: "In an honest, loving dialogue no one has to lose." Whatever pain is uncovered in the process of improving a relationship was there all along, and it can't heal until it's exposed to the light. It may hurt to expose the pain, but in the end it's the only path to healing and resolution.

So Loranna forged ahead. She told her mother about the times Lee's harsh criticism had left her feeling no better than a worm. She told her about the difficulty she had as a teenager believing that any boy could like someone as worthless as she must be. And about the complications her low self-esteem had created within her marriage.

Finally, when Loranna had said all she needed to, her mother began to speak. With tears rolling down her face Lee said, "I wanted so much to spare you the pain my parents caused me. I guess I didn't do a very good job, did I?" She went on to tell Loranna about the awful conditions she had endured when she was a child. Lee tried to verbalize her intense desire to do a better job with her children than her parents had and about her constant fear that she wasn't "doing it right" because of her lack of role models.

Lee gathered Loranna in her arms and cried, "I wanted to be the perfect mother. I thought that would somehow make up for all the bad things that happened to me when I was little. But all I accomplished was to make you feel like you weren't good enough because *I* never felt good enough and I kept trying to make both of us perfect. I'm so sorry."

Lee and Loranna wept together for a while. Before the weekend was over, they had agreed to put the past behind them and try to be "good enough" in the future.

Mothers and daughters trapped in the shaming cycle find themselves in a destructive spiral. In order to break out of that spiral, they need to begin a dialogue that will enable them to find new ground for their relationship. I like what Elizabeth O'Connor has to say about this process: "Dialogue is more than your giving me space to say my words, and my giving you space to say yours. It involves our listening. We are all very different. We cannot have dialogue unless we honor the differences. How can I build a bridge across the gulf between me and you unless I am aware of the gulf? How can I communicate with you unless I see how things look from your side?"[3]

Dialogue between mother and daughter can pave the way toward understanding and acceptance. It provides a way to expose secrets and address differences, an opportunity to lovingly express anger, disappointment, and pain so that solutions can be found. Dialogue makes room for vulnerability and accountability, both necessary ingredients in strengthening the integrity of the relationship. This kind of two-way communication leads to repair and resolution, hope, and resiliency—a new place of communion. I will offer some explicit instructions for beginning such a dialogue and resolving conflict in chapter eight.

IT CUTS BOTH WAYS

Many years ago I had a neighbor who never seemed to have a kind word to say about her mother. Marjorie had always been ashamed of Millie, a woman who had grown up in the rural south and barely made it through sixth grade before her mother died. She had been forced to drop out of school to care for her younger siblings and help out with farm chores. Millie had met and married Marjorie's father when she was just seventeen. The young couple had moved to a big city in the north to find work and raise a family.

Marjorie was always painfully aware of the fact that her mother didn't seem to fit in with city folk. She was ashamed of Millie's accent, her poor grammar, her southern cooking. Her mother couldn't please Marjorie no matter how hard she tried. The two women established an uneasy truce after

Marjorie married and moved away, but her yearly visits to her parents' home were always fraught with tension.

Then one year Millie was diagnosed with breast cancer. She had known for months that she had a lump in her breast, but had put off visiting the doctor, hoping it would go away. When Marjorie heard that Millie had been too shy to ask the doctor about it, she became incensed. How could her mother have allowed "silly modesty" to prevent her from seeking the help she needed? My neighbor was so upset when she received the news about her mother that I offered to drive her to the appointment she had made with her pastor.

Marjorie sat in her pastor's office complaining about her mother's "incompetence." He was a sensitive man who listened without condemnation while this woman spilled out her bitterness about her mother's "backward ways." Marjorie ended her diatribe by saying, "It's been this way all my life. All my life!"

Her pastor simply said, "And now those 'backward ways' are responsible for your mother's premature death, because she will die. You know that, don't you?"

Marjorie burst into tears. She buried her face in her hands and said to no one in particular, "How could she do this to me? Doesn't she know that I love her and I don't want to lose her?"

The pastor offered her his handkerchief as he asked, "How would she know you love her? Have you ever told her?"

Marjorie's looked up at him, stunned. Finally, she said, "Well, she must know I love her. She's my mother."

In a quiet voice he asked again, "*How* would she know?"

How unfortunate that it took Millie's impending death to bring her daughter to the realization that life is too short to "sweat the small stuff." When Marjorie got home that day she scheduled a trip to her parents' home. She told me later that she spent the last few weeks of Millie's life affirming her love for her mother.

My neighbor admitted she had to grind her teeth for a moment whenever Millie did one of the "typical" things that had always aggravated her so much. But Marjorie would remind herself that, in the larger scheme of things, a little "cornpone humor" or "a plate full of fish fried in enough lard to grease Route 66" wasn't terribly significant. She spent those weeks cooking her mother's favorite southern dishes and listening to her tell the same southern tales that she had scoffed at for so many years.

But this time Marjorie really listened. And this time she learned. She learned that each of her mother's stories had a point. Each story was meant to teach Marjorie what was really important in life. And this time she got the point. Marjorie came home a changed person. I could see the difference in the way she treated her husband and children. I could see it in the way she approached her church activities and life in general. More than once, I overheard Marjorie admonishing her children "not to sweat the small stuff."

Sometimes, we are our mother's or daughter's harshest judge. Marjorie was fortunate in a way. She had time to discover her error before it was too late to restore her relationship with her mother. Too many times, it doesn't happen that way.

BRIDGING THE GAP

Some of the dissimilarities between mothers and daughters stem from their distinct world views and life experiences. We live in a different era from the one in which our mothers grew up. This fact alone may yield different conclusions about how to live our lives.

Many of our mothers spent the majority of their lives nurturing their families, leaving little time and energy to pursue goals outside the home. I in no way mean to devalue the immensely important role of wife and mother, or to belittle those courageous women who choose to make this their life's work. While the contributions of a wife and mother remain invaluable, we are seeing more and more women modeling ways to use their gifts in a multitude of other pursuits—if they choose to do so. Women in today's world excel as doctors, lawyers, astronauts, teachers, administrators, politicians, counselors, editors, scientists—whether single or married, mothers or childless, young or old.

Many of our mothers believed that significant achievement in the broader world was beyond a woman's reach. Most members of the "younger generation" do not place those same limits upon themselves. Nevertheless, mothers often manage to project onto their daughters their own frame of reference and whatever limits are inherent within that box.

Anita came face-to-face with differences between her mother's world view and her own when she tried to discuss her career experiences. Although her mother had worked outside the home to provide additional income, Pearl never saw herself as a career woman and freely admits that her job brought her little personal satisfaction.

Anita and her husband notice a significant disparity in how their "shop talk" is greeted whenever they visit each set of parents. Gary is rewarded for carrying on his father's profession. He and his father interact freely about career issues in a respectful and slightly competitive spirit. But when Anita talks to her mother about her profession, she meets resistance rather than acceptance. Pearl pulls back, warns her not to work so hard, and reprimands her for being too involved in her career. Believing that her daughter's career takes too much energy, Pearl worries that the pressure is more than Anita can handle. Wishing that Anita and Gary would have children, she can't accept their decision to postpone parenthood so that Anita can continue to pursue her very satisfying career at this point in her life.

Anita loves her work and finds it energizing and fulfilling, but sharing this central part of herself raises walls between her and her mother. They both have difficulty understanding the other's point of view. Daughters of the modern world can envision a future for themselves which may be beyond their mother's wildest dreams. Unfortunately, in attaining those dreams, many of us have to work at editing our mothers' messages questioning our potential.

Many of our mothers grew up in a world where being a high achiever wasn't entirely "safe." Ambitious women were—and in many instances, still are—viewed with suspicion. They were the ones that culture dictated would be "old maids"—unloved and alone. While a mother's desire to safeguard her child may not be a malicious plot, those kinds of messages can nevertheless undermine a daughter's confidence about her abilities in the work place.

The same dynamic holds true when the scenario is reversed. My friend, Kate, has chosen to put her career on hold and remain at home while her children are young. Kate's mom is a devoted professional who can't imagine how her daughter keeps from "being bored to tears, stuck at home with nothing but rug-rats to talk to." Kate would love to call her mom at the office to share her delight over a child's first word or step, but she's learned not to act on that desire. It seems to Kate that her mother feigns delight "for about six seconds" and then begins to lecture her about how good it would be for her to "get out into the world and interact with adults."

One time a group of mothers gathered in my living room to talk about the inordinate strain they put on themselves and their daughters. Jane said that she has to be superwoman in order to feel okay about the fact that she's chosen to mix career and mothering. Hearing an internal message about being selfish and neglecting her family for the sake of her career, she feels guilty for enjoying work outside her home. In order to alleviate that guilt, Jane feels she must prove she's more than adequate in both roles. Consequently, she ends up working herself until she exhibits the constitution of a damp dishrag and must finally fall back and regroup.

Vastly different perspectives on life can lead to a serious breakdown in a mother-daughter relationship. Until we're able to see how things look from the other person's viewpoint, we will never be able to understand and accept the distinctive experiences that shape the way we each think, feel, and behave. Understanding does not develop through defending our point of view or trying to convince the other that we're right. Understanding comes through listening to one another so that we can know how things look through that person's eyes.

Sometimes, what we *really* need to understand is the unconscious set of expectations that has been erected either by ourselves or by our mothers. Identifying and discussing those underlying messages can be a big help in our efforts to deal with them in healthier ways. God wants to guide each of us according to his own plans and purposes. In doing so, we may have to cooperate in clearing away a lot of underbrush and hanging vines from our minds and hearts.

Sometimes, a mother with a strong personality inadvertently stifles her daughter, leaving her unsure of herself. A daughter grows up wondering how to emerge from the lengthy shadow cast by her dominant, successful mother.

Sally is a successful career woman who is very supportive of her daughter. Still, Kay's relationship with her mother remains troubled. Sally often told her daughter that she hoped Kay would "aspire to greater heights" than she ever dared to. Even as an adult, Kay isn't sure exactly what that means. But that message somehow keeps her paralyzed, afraid to try new things for fear they won't carry her high enough to please her mother.

Kay wants to please her mother, to stay close to her, to "make her proud." She finds herself taking on Sally's opinions even when she isn't comfortable with them because she fears her mother's disapproval. Kay says, "I struggle in my mind sometimes, and I try to decide what *I* really think—to allow myself to differ with her and withstand her quiet but clear judgment. I love her and want her to feel close to me, so I often voice agreement with her even when I'm not sure she's right."

Until Kay takes the risk to find out what Sally meant by "greater heights," she'll probably remain paralyzed. She may be surprised. Perhaps her mother simply meant that she hopes Kay will have access to a greater range of both personal and career choices. Such a dialogue would give Sally an opportunity to understand herself better by articulating what may have been, until then, a rather nebulous hope for Kay's future.

Both mother and daughter will learn more about themselves and each other when they can identify the unspoken messages behind the words of the past. Such an honest encounter can lead to even more provocative questions. Is it disloyal for a daughter to be more successful than her mother? If a mother is divorced, is it disloyal for her daughter to have a successful marriage? If a mother is a career woman, is it disloyal for her daughter to make more money or climb higher on the corporate ladder? Is Sally hoping that Kay will fulfill a dream that she was never able to realize for herself?

When we truly listen to what the other person has to say, this kind of dialogue can bring about great healing, as well as present an opportunity for immense growth for a mother, a daughter, and their relationship.

OUR MANY SELVES

Perhaps the difficulty some mothers have in truly affirming their daughters stems from an inability or unwillingness to accept all of the various facets of their personalities. I believe we often have trouble accepting ourselves for the very same reason.

Do you feel the need to hide certain parts of yourself from your mother? Do your own self-doubts cause you to put up a facade when you're with others, showing only those parts of your personality which you think they will find likeable? Are you confused by the fact that you seem to be able to conduct an argument all by yourself? During the past twenty years my students and clients have found it very helpful to get in touch with all of their inner voices. You may find it equally helpful.

My friend, Sherry, described her internal argument to me one day. She was being driven to distraction by the various "voices" in her head. One told her that her biological clock was ticking and she needed to have a baby as soon as possible. Another reminded her that she would be better off waiting until she could get her career better established before she considered taking time off to have a baby.

Then Sherry thought about her sister's new baby. Remembering how soft the baby felt and how wonderful he smelled made her feel hardly able to wait to have a baby of her own. But the internal voice that chimed in on the heels of that thought reminded her that babies aren't all warm fuzzies. Children add significant stresses to a marriage and perhaps she and her husband weren't ready for that.

My friend felt muddled and confused by all those conflicting "voices" in her head. Sherry's tendency in the past had been to pick the voice she felt was the most acceptable—to herself, her mother, her husband, her boss, and so forth—and ignore the others. But the resulting decisions were sometimes disastrous.

I asked Sherry, "How can you accept yourself if you don't listen to all the parts of yourself? Each of your internal 'selves' is voicing a legitimate concern. Why not take the time to listen to them all, even the ones that seem less acceptable, and then come to a well thought out decision that will be the most satisfactory?"

You may not be weighing the advisability of having a baby right now, but I can almost guarantee that you come up against this same problem in regard to other important decisions. Where do all these voices come from? Why are some of their messages contradictory and confusing? How can you value input from the voices that seem to be undesirable or "bad"?

One voice told Sherry that she liked her marriage just as it was and didn't want to share her husband with a child. In dismissing that voice as selfish and petty, she could have missed a valuable signal about her readiness to be a mother. Perhaps turning a deaf ear to that message would be to miss an important clue about an insecure marriage relationship, with or without children.

Perhaps the idea that you are a multifaceted person with a different voice for each of those facets is new to you. You may even have an aversion to the idea. Richard Schwartz refers to the "myth of the monolithic self" which seems to suggest that people must be "consistent unitary individuals who know their own minds."[4] Nothing could be farther from reality.

Even though Transactional Analysis psychotherapy presents some difficulties, Eric Berne, in his book, *Transactional Analysis in Psychotherapy*, has added to our understanding of our various selves by identifying the nurturing parent, critical parent, adult, and child parts of ourselves.[5] The messages we receive from these various parts are most often triggered by certain situations. For example, at a party we may be more likely to display our spontaneous, playful child-part. At a business meeting the responsible, forthright adult-part of us may make a persuasive speech in order to affect a decision. The condemning parent-part may kick into gear when our husband is delinquent in completing the household chores he agreed to do.

However you choose to name the various parts of yourself, you may find it interesting to identify which voice most often interacts with your mother. Laurel Lee, in her charming book, *Signs of Spring*, makes this observation about herself: "A peculiar chemistry takes place at the door of my parents' house. Somehow, between turning the simulated brass doorknob and stepping onto the beige carpet, my molecules lose their structure. I stand in need of their reconstruction."[6]

Do you find, as Laurel Lee did, that the child part of you is the one that most frequently interacts with your mother? What other voices do you hear? Is there one particular part of you that you would prefer to give more of a say in your mother-daughter relationship?

Some mothers make it clear to us—sometimes subtly, sometimes not so subtly—that they find certain parts of us unacceptable. Some of us react to those messages by refraining from showing that side of ourselves to our mothers. Most of us, however, eventually find that it is simply too costly to be that untrue to ourselves. One of the exercises at the end of this chapter may help you to decide how you can help your mother accept all the various facets of your personality.

GRACEFULLY ACCEPTING DIFFERENCES

When we respectfully acknowledge the ways in which we are unlike our mothers or other family members, we can find ways to be accepting of each other without trying to force others into meeting our expectations. One way to go about this is to make a list of the things you believe your mother expects of you. Then make a second list composed of the things you expect from yourself.

For example, you may think that your mother is pleased with your church activities because she expects you to be actively involved in the church. But, how do *you* feel about it? Have you established a personal faith or is your involvement in church a way of gaining her acceptance? When you're clear about your own expectations you'll be better able to be true to yourself. That, in turn, will enable you to accept others more graciously.

When Virginia's mother asked her why she didn't have a traditional picture of Jesus hanging in her house instead of the modern Madonna and Child sculpture, Virginia responded in a non-defensive way. She told her mother that the sculpture represented God's love for the world in the incarnation event. Instead of reacting to her mother's slightly judgmental statement, she took a direction that deepened their discussion. She resisted defending differences about aesthetic preferences, and turned the situation into an opportunity for sharing with her mother on a deeper level.

My Aunt May once told me how hurt she was when her daughter decided to change denominations. Jennifer became involved in a liturgical dance group in the church she attended. The notion that dance could be used in worship was quite foreign to her mother. But Aunt May kept her uneasiness to herself. She decided she would rather support Jennifer's active pursuit of her faith than express her discomfort about liturgical dance.

When Jennifer invited her mother to a Sunday morning service where she was to perform an Easter liturgical dance, Aunt May went with some reservation. But she kept an open mind and was profoundly moved by the experience. May felt assured that her daughter's adoration of God through dramatic expression brought her closer to her Lord. Jennifer's desire to share this expression of her faith with her mother brought them closer to one another, and May's ability to keep an open mind beforehand paved the way for that special closeness to develop.

ACCEPTING OUR WOUNDED SELVES

When we were children, we had little say in the way we were raised. As adults, however, we can choose to become all that God means for us to be. We can choose to make changes in our mother-daughter relationship. We can choose to seek nurturance and affirmation from others. Or we can do both. In God's kingdom, there are no hopeless cases. But God leaves the choices to us.

If you felt unaccepted by your mother as you were growing up, you may wish to arrange a time when you can calmly and lovingly tell your mother about your feelings. Or you can tell your mother how sorry you are for having judged her so harshly in the past. That sort of encounter can help to heal hurts and create a climate for change within the mother-daughter relationship.

Whether or not you choose to make changes in your relationship with your mother, you can consciously seek a maternal figure with whom to interact. Someone from your church or club or workplace may fulfill that role for you. My friend, Eleanor, whose mother is mentally ill, has chosen a few women as role models and "affirmers" in her life. She appreciates one of her special female friends for her spontaneity and artistic ability, another for her wisdom and analytical thinking, and another for her calm faith in the Lord. Each of these women is pleased by this woman's choice to make her a part of her life. Eleanor is receiving from them what her mother was never able to give her.

The truth is, we always receive partial rather than total acceptance from our mothers and other family members. It is only in Christ Jesus that we are completely accepted just as we are. We are created in God's image and loved unconditionally by God. Knowing that, how can we refuse to accept ourselves? We are free to rest in the Lord, refusing to be ashamed of who God made us. We don't have to reach perfection in order to be acceptable.

All of us make mistakes. All of us make unwise choices and violate others' trust at times. All of us need to be forgiven. That's why God's Son came to die for us. In a healthy home forgiveness is freely given. Our mothers can model forgiveness by teaching us to ask for and receive forgiveness from the one we've wronged and from God. They can release us from the shame of our mistakes until we learn to release ourselves. They can reassure us that we're still acceptable for who we are, regardless of anything we may have done.

Cindy told me about a time when she blatantly lied to her mother. She felt she had committed the ultimate sin—that it would destroy their relationship. That evening, Cindy's mother came into her room and said, "I forgive you, Cindy. Do you forgive me?" Both of them experienced a renewed tenderness toward one another. Without any sense of judgment, they simply recognized that the lie had come between them and forgiveness was needed on both sides.

Forgiveness is a powerful source of healing. When forgiveness is withheld, we often feel unacceptable and ashamed. When freely granted, it helps us to accept ourselves and others, even when we fail. Forgiveness is the most direct route to restoration.

Some mothers are able to let go of their expectations and fully accept us as we are. Others don't necessarily approve of everything we do, but they love us regardless of what we do. Some few will never accept us. Whatever our particular situation, we can seek acceptance from others who can affirm and support us just as we are. Ultimately, their acceptance coupled with our awareness of God's acceptance can help free us to be ourselves.

That's what happened at a women's workshop I attended last fall. Fifty women sat in a circle, all strangers. The workshop leaders had taken us through the four major developmental stages of a woman's life; the child; the teenager; the mature adult; and the aging woman. It had been a day filled with laughter, tears, frivolity, and sharing.

Focused on our personal pain, we grew silent when the workshop leaders asked us what childhood messages had wounded us. One by one, the women began sharing wounding comments. "You're too fat to play tennis." "You can't do that; you're a woman." "Don't wear those tight pants; you look just like your mother." "It's all right for your brother but not for you." "You can't reason; you're a girl." "You wear your emotions on your sleeve." As we listened to one after another, we felt the seriousness of the injuries we had suffered.

Then we were invited to take a brightly colored piece of cloth from the center of the circle and bind it around the place on our body that had been wounded by those messages. Slowly women got up from their seats, took a rag, and bound up their own wounds. You could hear a pin drop as we sat together in that room surveying one another's wounds, taking in each other's pain. Our bodies were bound in various places: around the head; over the eyes; across the mouth; on an arm, a leg, a foot; across the chest; around the heart, the stomach, the hips, the buttocks, the thigh; sometimes down the entire front of the body. Our empathy for each other and a recognition of our commonality produced goose bumps.

Then we each found a partner, shared with her our particular wound, and slowly unbound one another. In this simple ceremony of healing and release, our wounds were accepted as real and we were accepted—and found acceptable—as wounded persons. We laughed and cried as we freed each other from our bondage. We found strength in our acceptance of one another as women.

This is one way self-acceptance can bring about healing. Our wounds can become enlightening messages of strength. When women—especially mothers and daughters—accept one another, they will be able to accept themselves. And acceptance is where love begins.

Exercises

1. Does a gulf exist between you and your mother? Identify that gulf in specific details so you can be more aware of the way it comes between you.

2. Are the personality differences between you and your mother accepted, valued, and affirmed? What can you do to help this happen?

3. Once you have identified your own inner voices, consider introducing them to your mother. Which facets of your personality does she accept and which does she disapprove of? Does this affect your own ability to accept those parts of yourself?

4. Give an example from your childhood when you felt guilty about breaking a rule. How did you resolve your guilt and what were the consequences of that experience?

5. Give an example of a time when you felt a sense of shame for who you are. What were the circumstances? How did you face your shame and get beyond it?

6. Are you still a perfectionist trying to be measure up, or have you admitted and accepted your human failings? What does it mean to you to be fully accepted, just as you are, in Christ Jesus?

7. Identify your wounded self. Tie a cloth around the location of your wounds. Write or talk out loud about your injuries. When you're ready, unbind your wounds, allowing for healing to take place in a silent meditation. Allow yourself to receive God's warm, comforting embrace. Ask God to transform your wounds from weakness into strength.

SIX

~~~~~~

Personality Traits and Mothering Styles

I RECENTLY OBSERVED A YOUNG MOTHER interacting with her new baby in the doctor's waiting room. The mother seemed inexperienced and excitable, the baby more lethargic and inactive. Mother's cooing initially received a nice response. However, her baby turned her head away at a certain point as if to say, "Give me a break!"

The mother paid no attention to this subtle cue and continued to stimulate the newborn. The baby, typically a captive audience, could not ignore or escape the mother's interaction, became irritated and started crying, as if to beg, "Do something calming!" Instead, this rather high-strung mother bounced her baby up and down, causing more irritation, whereupon baby escalated her demands by crying harder. The relationship was already off to a bad start.

We have thus far seen many common elements within the mother-daughter relationship, like our need for bonding and separation and for acceptance. While each pairing works out the particulars in different ways, those kinds of needs always remain the same. Other facets within the relationship can vary greatly, depending on an individual's personal temperament and preferences.

For example, each baby needs an optimal amount of physical and emotional stimulation. One with a relaxed temperament requires more arousal from her mother to help her respond to her outer environment. A baby with an excitable temperament, on the other hand, needs more soothing in order to be more in touch with her internal world. On the other side of the relationship, an excitable mother may overstimulate her baby, not giving her sufficient time to be quiet. A mother who tends to be too relaxed may understimulate and fail to give her baby sufficient arousal. Mothers and daughters of *similar* temperaments face the potential danger of either mutual overarousal or underarousal.

The dynamics of these various styles of relating begin to show up very early in life. In fact, studies in infant behavior have shown that each mother-daughter pair establishes a distinct style of interaction.

I do not believe that any one personality or mothering style can be held up as the perfect model for all to follow. God delights in diversity when it comes to creating human beings. Usually of more crucial importance is how well each mother and daughter duo mesh in terms of their unique styles of relating to one another. The issue is one of a "good fit," the trick being to promote the right combination by taking into consideration the individual styles of both individuals. Establishing that delicate balance of connectedness and separation often provides a visible litmus test for the effectiveness of specific mothering styles.

Mother and baby each play a vital part in the bonding process, but because the mother is more mature, she must usually adapt herself to her daughter's needs. Regardless of her own temperament, the adult is expected to be flexible enough to respond in ways that are appropriate to each unique child. A baby feels secure when her mother is attuned to her needs for both attachment and distance. When mother and daughter achieve a good fit, the relationship proceeds more smoothly; when they don't, difficulties often arise.[1]

As time goes on, mothers who are particularly good at connecting may have more trouble separating from their daughters. Because they have such a strong natural tendency to merge with loved ones, their daughters often feel smothered. When the daughter attempts to move away, the mother feels threatened. On the other hand, if a mother is unable to establish a close connection, her daughter usually grows up feeling isolated and rejected.

Establishing the right balance between connection and separation during the teenage years can be far more problematic. A teenager typically values input from and interaction with her peers more than from her mother. Mothers and daughters who are constant companions during the teenage years are likely to encounter trouble with emotional distancing later on. The teen years, in particular, require mothers to perform a difficult but necessary tightrope-walk.

HAVE YOU GOT A MATCH?

Gretchen's two adult daughters have extremely different temperaments. Wendy is very similar to her mother; both are "laid back" about life. They feel warm and close when together but are equally content when apart. With lives of their own, Gretchen and Wendy are comfortable with the balance they have achieved between connection and separation.

It's just the opposite with the other daughter. Justine is a rather high-strung and energetic person. Continually exasperated, Gretchen complains that she doesn't have a clue as to how to relate to her. Notably, their clashes are the only times they connect with one another since their separations last for months. Their different temperaments keep them from coming together in a healthy way.

Finding the right balance of connectedness and separateness requires that we first recognize differences in temperament. Then, with patience and flexibility we can begin to find ways to make our differences work for us. Finding the right fit is a challenge, but an improved relationship is worth the effort.

Too much connection. "My mother is a mirror. When I look at her, I see myself in her image." Kelly feels like she is little more than an extension of her mother, Donna. She doesn't feel like she has a self. At the mature age of thirty-seven, this grown woman panics at the thought of shopping for her own clothes. Donna has purchased everything that hangs in her daughter's closet, despite the fact that Kelly hates most of the styles her mother chooses for her!

Kelly can't find the courage to tell her mother to stop because that would mean she would have to buy clothes for herself. The dependency that has developed between them entangles them both. Donna hasn't the slightest idea how angry Kelly is, although she senses her daughter's disdain from time to time. They seldom express love to each other as they move through the cold, routinized patterns of obligation, dependency, and resentment.

If a mother has no separate life of her own, she will be tempted to be overly-involved with her daughter. Mother feels invested in every aspect of her daughter's life, from the way she looks to the way she performs. The illusion of closeness keeps the necessary separation from developing. In such a case, the daughter seldom feels free to make a move either, because she remains just as trapped in this long established pattern.

Mother and daughter keep step with each other to an old waltz. Granted, they may step on each other's toes now and again, but neither suggests that they change partners or find a new dance. Since they can see no graceful way out of their predicament, the music plays on and on.

When a mother can't see any possible avenues to the establishment of an individual identity for herself—whatever the reason—she finds it almost impossible to accept her daughter's desire to individuate. If she senses that her daughter may be feeling exasperated or smothered, she may unconsciously arrange to cut her daughter down to size, shredding her self-esteem so that her daughter won't feel competent enough to leave her. It's a lonely mother who tries to bind her daughter to her for life.

A mother may keep her daughter bound to her by forming an exclusive coalition, which can tend to keep Dad out of the picture. When a daughter becomes her mother's sole connection, both the husband/wife and father/daughter relationships are disrupted. Carline's story portrays such an unfortunate dynamic:

> I felt like I existed to please my mother. I was so anxious to do what she wanted me to that I never had a chance to get close to my dad. I regret to this day that he died before I could find a way to connect with him. Mom made our relationship so sacred. She wanted me all to herself.
>
> I cringe when I remember the day I arranged to meet mother for lunch at a local coffee shop. My dad happened to overhear our conversation and showed up by surprise to join us. His eager look and the twinkle in his eye made me realize how much he was looking forward to being with us.
>
> Mom raked him over the coals for intruding on our special mother-daughter time. Dad was devastated and I was embarrassed for him. I'm sad when I think about how much I would have liked being with him and yet I suc-

cumbed to my mother's control. I was mad at her, and mad at myself for the wedge my mother and I had driven between my dad and us. I never did get through to him about how much he meant to me.

To this day I am superconscious of wanting to please others. I'm afraid to speak out in a group because I think I'll be judged and criticized. I have very strong opinions, but even when there's opportunity to speak I keep my mouth shut. I'm sure my ideas will be disregarded just as my dad was always disregarded. He wasn't acceptable, so I must not be acceptable. My stomach starts to churn when I want to speak so I keep quiet, feeling hurt and angry afterwards that I didn't say what I wanted to say.

My mother and dad died years ago, and now I'm trying to find ways to feel better about myself. I've been in a small group of women for the past four years and I've begun to express some of the feelings I've kept to myself for so many years. It's still difficult for me, but when I do speak up I feel better about myself. The group is willing to hear me out and I do experience acceptance there. But there are still times when I hesitate because this voice inside me says I'm unacceptable.

Too much separation. Cynthia's mother was mentally ill, emotionally unavailable, distant, inconsistent, and impossible to relate to during her daughter's childhood years. Cynthia became a mother to her mother. Expected to perform like an adult before she had started kindergarten, this growing girl can't remember a time when she wasn't trying to meet her mother's needs.

As all children do in such circumstances, Cynthia felt guilty when she failed to parent her mother appropriately. This impossible position for a child also caused a lot of confusion in her relationship with her father. From an early age, Cynthia served as a substitute wife for her father and took on much of the responsibility for keeping the household running. She tried to meet his emotional needs by being a sounding board and providing encouragement, at an age when her greatest concern should have been whether or not she would be invited to a classmate's slumber party.

As often results in families where this sort of confusion persists, Cynthia's father/daughter relationship became still more unhealthy. Eventually, her father began pressuring her to meet his sexual needs too. Burdened beyond her years with the utterly inappropriate task of satisfying her mother's emotional needs and her father's sexual demands, this young girl began to feel crazy.

In reality, Cynthia's situation *was* crazy because she had become a pseudo-adult long before her time. She couldn't separate herself from her parents because their demands bound her to them. But at the same time, she wasn't connected either because they were emotionally unavailable to her. Cynthia had been emotionally abandoned. In a very real sense, she sacrificed her life for theirs.

Unfortunately, distressing stories like this one are more common than you might think. Is it any wonder that Cynthia doesn't want to be a parent today? Is it any surprise that she struggles with depression, migraine headaches, and an eating disorder? She has battled for years with the impact of her topsy-turvy family system. The one nurturing person in Cynthia's life was the black nanny who cared for her during the first few years. The trust she developed as a result of this woman's unconditional love gave her the ability to trust a therapist once she was an adult.

Eventually Cynthia came to recognize the loss, neglect, and abuse she had suffered as a child. Her therapist became a kind of surrogate mother for a time. She had finally captured the attention of a consistent, loving woman who could help her recapture some of the stages of growth she had missed during childhood. In time and with love, Cynthia grew to be an emotionally healthy adult.

Achieving balance. Even though many of us have never had to be a full-time mother to our mothers, we may have experienced a time when our mothers needed us to nurture them. I remember the time it happened for me, immediately following the death of Grandmother Rummelt. Even as a grown woman myself, I was surprised and rather shocked to see my mother react so emotionally to her mother's death. For the first time in my life I realized how dependent she had been on her own mother. Now that her mother was dead, she clung to me for comfort.

Letting my mother depend on me felt very strange and unnatural. However, it did help me face the issue of our own connection-separation balance. Had I really separated as much as I thought I had? Was I ready for her to need my support or did I still assume she would always mother me? I realized that appropriate dependence on one another in moments of need doesn't negate our separateness. In fact, it is only when we are sufficiently individuated from each other that we can give to each other in a helpful, interdependent way.

We all experience the natural ebb and flow of connection and separation throughout our lives. As adult daughters we can offer strength to our mothers when they need us to be there for them. As our mothers age and we mature, the relationship should become more reciprocal. What started out as a one-way, unconditional love from mother to daughter grows into a mutual covenant of commitment.

When our mothers become increasingly vulnerable with age, the tables may turn and they may become dependent on us. That, too, is a normal part of the life cycle which I will discuss further in chapter eleven. If a mother has helped her child to arrive at a balance between connection and separation in the earlier stages of her development, that balance will support such a turnabout in the later stages of life.

MOTHER, THIRD PERSON OUT!

An exclusive relationship with father, making mother the outsider, can also disrupt the family. When Sandy heard that I was writing a book on mothers and daughters, she came to my office to tell me her story. As a child, she became enmeshed with her father, a recovering alcoholic, and in the process became estranged from her mother.

Sandy felt very satisfied with the care and attention she received from her father, but found it increasingly more difficult to relate to her mother. That exclusive relationship with her father also caused a breach between Sandy and her siblings. It's as if she had all of her daddy and he had all of her so that no one else could receive anything from either of them.

After her parents divorced, Sandy chose to live with her father and remained estranged from the rest of her family. She didn't realize how dysfunctional this arrangement was until her father died unexpectedly of a heart attack four years later. Suddenly, Sandy realized that she had lost not only her father but the rest of her family as well. Now she was totally alone, without family support.

Shortly after her father's death Sandy found herself facing a series of problems. In desperation she called her mother, who had been working the twelve-step Al-Anon program. Sandy's mom listened compassionately to her daughter's plea for help, but declined to rescue her. She suggested that Sandy make a list of her problems and start tackling them one at a time. She told Sandy to call when she solved the first one so that they could celebrate together.

Sandy was angered by her mother's response, but took her advice and tackled the first problem on her list. When that problem was solved, her mother, true to her word, celebrated with her. Looking back, Sandy can see that her mother supported her in a way which forced her to reach inside herself to find the strength to deal with her own problems.

It has been a slow process but Sandy and her mother have established a solid relationship. They have gradually discovered how much they share in common, especially their interest in psychology and in helping others. Now the two of them work as a team, giving workshops within their community on mother-daughter relationships.

Sandy admits that she became estranged from her mother as a result of her own choice to be in an exclusive relationship with her father, although the family dynamic and the husband/wife relationship were also contributing factors. No dysfunctional relationship develops in a vacuum. Sandy received benefits from her exclusive relationship with her father, but at the heavy cost of rejecting her femaleness by becoming her father's substitute son. Her strong focus on career left no room for marriage or children. Happily, Sandy is now recapturing her femininity.

Excluding either the mother or father from our support system causes disruption in the normal connection/separation process. We need to strike a balance between the two.

WE ALL HAVE STYLE

At the beginning of this chapter, I suggested that each baby daughter is unique, requiring mothers to adjust to their own individual temperaments. It is just as true that a mother's temperament helps to determine her style of mothering regardless of how much she may manage to adjust to her baby. As adult women, we are challenged to discover these differences so that we can have a mature relationship with our mothers.

I would like to discuss four basic parenting styles: neglectful, authoritarian, permissive, and authoritative. As I describe each one, try to identify your mother's predominant style, keeping in mind that most mothers utilize various combinations throughout their years of parenting.

Remember that a mother's style may change abruptly due to a personal or family circumstance or crisis, such as a death in the family, a serious illness, or a new job outside the home. Whatever the case, it will be helpful to you to identify the style your mother used with you during different times in your life.

The neglectful style. A neglectful mothering style is especially painful, because she is not adequately invested emotionally nor does she provide consistent guidance. The neglectful mother is often trapped in an emotional state (possibly due to deep depression, physical illness, alcoholism, etc.) that keeps her distant and cut off from her children.

This person was herself most likely neglected as a child so that she possesses little knowledge or skill as a mother. In this sort of family, it tends to be "every one for herself." Some children never receive even the basics of life, such as adequate food, clothing, nurture, or shelter. Even if they survive, they pay an immense price in terms of emotional stability and health.

Henrietta was one such child who learned to fend for herself at an early age. Living a meager existence within her own home, she was sometimes hungry and without warm enough clothing. Lacking basic care and nurturance, Henrietta naturally grew up believing that the world was a frightening place.

The authoritarian style. The authoritarian mother is the ultimate authority. She sets a high standard for what is right and punishes any wrong. She does not believe in giving her child too much attention, for fear it will go to her head. Such a mother is generally stingy with her rewards for good behavior, but expects her child to behave precisely as she wishes.

Kay lived under the edict of an authoritarian mother. She

grew up knowing that rules were more important than she was. Mother dictated how things were to be done and expected daughter to carry them out down to the last jot and tittle. When Kay deviated from any regulation—even in an innocent, child-like way—she received harsh punishment. She learned to keep the peace by obeying the rules but couldn't conceive of a healthy, loving relationship with this unkind woman.

The permissive style. The permissive mother is one who frequently brags about her child and her behavior, but seldom points out areas that need improvement. She often gives her child excessive freedom to make her own decisions while providing little direction or guidance. This mother tends to believe that a child will find her own limits if given enough rope. She lets her child do what she wants so as to bring out the child's natural creativity.

While the permissive mother fervently believes in her child's great potential, the child often feels overwhelmed by the responsibility for delivering on that potential without benefit of any specific direction or guidance.

Clara was the envy of all her friends. They thought she got away with murder. With the freedom to do as she jolly well pleased, she seemed to have it made. Yet Clara felt overwhelmed by the lack of structure and chaos in her life. Instead of a warm, indulgent, and lax relationship with her mother, this young girl wanted and needed assistance in making life decisions. She needed to be taught problem-solving skills that she could carry into her adult life. Clara usually felt bewildered more than carefree.

The authoritative style. Believing that it's her responsibility to guide, the authoritative mother provides correction and direction along with adequate support. She develops an emotional relationship with her child and values the child as a unique person. This kind of mother is quick to acknowledge and encourage her child's giftedness and achievements, yet not afraid to be firm and clear when it comes to setting guidelines. She expects her children to be accountable for their actions.

Molly could always count on her mother to bring perspective to any problem and to suggest direction whenever Molly asked for it. But her mother also affirmed Molly's ability to make her own choices, even when she asked for advice. Molly's mom didn't criticize her for making mistakes but rather showed her ways to learn from them. As a result, Molly grew up to be a responsible, secure adult.

Social scientists concur that of these four, the authoritative style is the most desirable. The best environment for the growth and learning of a child is one which provides both firm guidance and support. Because they've experienced either excessive or insufficient discipline, children who grow up in authoritarian or permissive homes generally tend to be rebellious. Neglected children are least likely to reach their full potential.[2]

BUT THAT'S NOT ALL

Some mothers focus on providing a **model** for their children to emulate. Believing that her children would learn best by observing, Kyang-Soo's mother lived out the values she embraced, rather than simply talking about them. Assuming that standards for behavior are assimilated through close proximity, she carried her babies next to her during the daily work hours and slept nearby. Her children became very familiar with their mother's practical, down-to-earth activities and deeply revered family traditions. As she grew Kyang-Soo was able to incorporate them into a personal guide for living.

Gaby's mother primarily took on the role of a **teacher** by describing and defining everything for her children during their growing years. She read books, gave them tid-bits of information when they were together, helped them solve problems, and took them to interesting places so that they could learn about life. Her cognitive approach developed out of a desire to teach her children all of the particulars about their environment.

Enforcement of the rules often involved long explanations for the punishment. When her mother's teaching turned to preaching, Gaby grew weary of it in short order. Her mother was logical and reasonable but seemed detached. While Gaby valued that objectivity when she made decisions, she often wished her mother was more emotionally available. As she grew older, the discrepancy between what her mother taught and the way she lived eventually caused Gaby to challenge her mother's authority.

The **nurturer** does a great job telling her children how much she loves them, complimenting and affirming them without hesitation. She enjoys heart-to-heart talks and being close. But, sometimes this kind of mother nurtures her children to death. "Smother-love" can begin to set in. Jan enjoyed the frequent hugs she received from her mom as a child, but feels it's excessive now that she's an adult. She feels embarrassed at the age of thirty to be referred to as "little Janny" or "my baby."

The nurturer's zeal to protect her child—especially when that need is long past—can be problematic. Jan flinches every time her mother tries to entice her to move back home "where's she'll be safe." Because her mother's actions are often triggered by her emotions, she blows things out of proportion, over-reacting to news items from the metropolitan area where her daughter lives. Jan's mother tends to idealize life on the one hand or react to minor mishaps as if they were catastrophes on the other.

Again, most mothers combine these various emphases to

produce a multitude of differences. Most people learn their parenting style from their own parents, without taking time to evaluate the negative and positive impact it has on their own children. If a mother can identify her own primary style, she can work at making any adjustments necessary to improve her relationship with her children. All parents have a flat side that needs rounding out—a blind spot until someone lovingly points it out so they can change.

For example, a mother who utilizes a teaching style can learn to ease up on her preaching and concentrate more on modeling the behaviors she espouses. The mother who models, on the other hand, will enhance her impact when she takes time to talk about the important values which guide her life. While the laissez-faire mother will benefit from giving her daughter more instruction and guidance, the authoritarian mother can expand her narrow focus on discipline by listening to and supporting her daughter in more personal ways.

DIFFERENT STROKES FOR DIFFERENT FOLKS

Other various personality traits also contribute to the mother-daughter relationship. Four prominent traits as identified on the Myers-Briggs Type Indicator can especially affect the delicate equilibrium between mother and daughter.[3]

The **extravert** tends to be outgoing, expressive, outspoken, and likes to be around people—the life of the party. Communication skills are her forte and interpersonal relationships her passion. An extraverted person is typically on the go, participating in many activities outside the home, volunteering, and chairing committees. Her world is often in a whirl because she keeps so many irons in the fire. It's hard for this type of person to relax since she's usually thinking about the next event on her schedule.

At times the extraverted mother may overpower her daughter by trying to be overly helpful. Laura always felt like she was playing second-fiddle to her outgoing mom. When her girlfriends came to visit, her mother took over the conversation and became the center of attention. Laura began to wonder if her friends came to see her or her mom. She tended to hold back when her mother was present, resenting Mom but also depending on her in social situations.

Finally, Laura began to speak up for herself. She asked her mother to back off, to slow down, and to let her take the initiative. Mother learned to monitor her extraverted personality, giving her daughter a chance to blossom on her own. And Laura gradually learned to be more socially interactive by watching her mother and following her lead.

On the other hand, the **introvert** tends to be more inner-directed and quiet. Preferring solitude to being with people, she likes to spend time alone. Since interacting with others feels more like a chore, she keeps more to herself even when she's in a group.

Linda's mother was more introverted. She recalls how her mom arranged private times with her, away from outside interference. They took quiet walks and had private lunches together. Being more attuned to an internal world, her mother considered what was going on inside of Linda to be of utmost importance. She was good at reflecting her daughter's thoughts and feelings back to her in a non-intrusive way.

Even though Linda cherishes this intimate side to their relationship, she has hesitated to ask her mother to attend social events because it would be uncomfortable for her. When they talked about this dilemma, Linda's mother faced her inhibitions, stretched herself, and began attending some of these important occasions in her daughter's life.

Obvious problems can develop between different combinations of extraverted and introverted personalities. For example, it's natural for an introverted daughter to hold back, responding slowly to a new situation. In exasperation, the extraverted mother is likely to take over when this occurs. In contrast, when an extraverted daughter approaches an unfamiliar situation without hesitation, her extraverted mother takes pride in her while an introverted mother may feel intimidated.

To consider another example, an introverted daughter tends to prefer a quiet, one-on-one, reflective interaction with her mother while the extraverted mother wants to spend her time with her daughter *doing* something. Because she is bowled over by external stimulus, the introverted daughter typically declines invitations from her extraverted mother for those events, leaving both with an "out of sync" feeling.

Besides extraversion and introversion, two other personality traits identified by the Myers-Briggs Type Indicator affect a person's approach to parenting. Mothers who prefer **structure** will generally have a more precise parenting style. This type of person values predictability and is happiest when life proceeds according to schedule. It's important for her to have things settled. Any kind of disorder disturbs her because it causes her to feel out of control. When things are up in the air she's upset until they're straightened out.

This mother prefers to plan ahead, likes closure, and usually completes what she starts. She is decisive and can be rigid or pushy when she wants to get something done. Daughters of highly structured mothers may feel inadequate when they don't meet their mothers' standards. On the other hand, a daughter who highly values structure can sometimes "out-structure" her mother.

Millie follows in her mother's footsteps when it comes to this particular personality trait. She's so structured that her rigidity sometimes keeps others at a distance. Millie's glad to be single and living alone because she has no one underfoot intruding upon her routines. When she prepares for a trip she keeps copious lists of things to do and pack. When Millie and her mother travel together, they consistently butt heads because their elaborate systems don't always mesh. These clashes cause major disruptions in their relationship because neither one of them is terribly willing to bend.

On the other hand, an opposite personality type values **spontaneity**. This kind of mother has a passion for thinking outside the boundaries of structure. They are generally visionaries, mavericks who aren't afraid to take risks or to look foolish when they do something out of the ordinary. They look for opportunities for themselves and their daughters to go beyond their perceived capacity in order to reach their creative potential.

Rita laughs about the fact that her mother refused to wear anything "off the rack." A trendsetter with a true gift for combining colors and styles from her wardrobe into ingenious outfits, Doreen insisted on designing all of her own clothes. Rita grew up believing that the worst thing in the world was to be like everybody else. Her mother's creative ideas for home decor impressed everyone who entered their house.

Doreen was intrigued by new ideas and approaches to life. Rita thoroughly appreciated her mother's ability to ask provocative questions when she came to her with a problem. She had a way of helping Rita gain an inner understanding of what was right for her. "She believed in my intuition and had a wonderful optimism about relying on my inner wisdom to develop my own life."

Sometimes, however, Rita wanted more concrete guidance from her mother. During her teens, she wanted specific advice about setting limits with her boyfriends. Also, Rita felt disappointed when her mother couldn't accept her desire to be more like her peers rather than to do her own thing. As an adult, she often wished her mother would be more understanding about her choice of an "ordinary" mate and a traditional home.

As you see, each of these four personality variables has its negative and positive points. A mother will naturally gravitate toward a daughter who exhibits a like temperament because she approaches life in a similar manner. Mothers and daughters who have opposite temperaments will naturally confront each other more often than their like-minded counterparts.

During their adult years, daughters need to work together with their mothers to achieve a mutually satisfying relationship. Respecting differences in personality traits challenges both mother and daughter to reach beyond their natural tendencies in order to come together in respectful ways.

WHERE DO WE GO FROM HERE?

The various ingredients that go into a mother's parenting style makes her unique. Daughters are just as unique. Our differing personalities are determined by our genetic make-up along with our socialization process. When they are mixed and matched, these styles can be regarded as complementary or disparate depending on one's attitude.

Our ongoing interaction with our mothers continues to shape us. Therefore, the more we can understand our differences as well as our similarities, the better we will know how to relate to each other as adult women. Our aim is to discover that just-right blend for our own mother-daughter relationship. Such a goal requires a concerted effort by both parties to transcend our uniqueness and achieve a satisfying harmony.

Parenting styles can be altered to achieve a better balance and personality traits can be tempered to achieve greater compatibility. As in a marriage, learning to mesh with another person is a matter of accepting and adapting to one another's unique styles. Since each mother and daughter has her own unique personality, the important factor is their willingness to respond to one another in mutually beneficial ways.

Perhaps the ideas in this chapter have convinced you that some of your conflicts with your mother may be due to a difference in styles and your approach to life. Take heart. With a little patience and understanding, this is generally one of the easiest relational problems to solve. Once you have worked through the following exercises, try making some concrete plans to implement a change in your approach to your mother-daughter relationship.

Exercises

1. Think about an early connection experience, a time when you felt especially warm and close to your mother. Next, bring to mind an early childhood experience of separation, like the day you went off to summer camp. Do you recognize any common themes in these experiences that influence the way you attach and separate from others today? Do you seek out persons in your life who have a calming or stimulating influence in your life?

2. Do you currently experience a good balance of attachment and separation with your mother? How would you like to change it? Would she agree with your evaluation? If not, what can you do to help her see things from your perspective?

3. Did you ever get into an exclusive relationship with either parent? If so, how did it affect your life?

4. Identify your mother's primary parenting style and tell how it meshed or clashed with your personality. What might you do to modify established parenting patterns that disrupt your current relationship? How can you let her know what you need from her in your adult interaction?

5. What temperaments did you and your mother bring to your relationship (extravert/introvert and structured/spontaneous)? How did particular similarities or differences specifically affect your interactions? How have you come to resolve the differences?

6. What are you currently doing to transcend the unique differences between you and your mother so that, together, you can fill out the flat side of your relationship and find harmony?

SEVEN

The Circle of Love and Hate: What Happens with Unresolved Anger

Alas, too late I stumbled upon what you expected of me.
"Why didn't you know?" you ask. And I reply, "How could I?"
Do I read minds? Do I own a crystal ball?
If I had been the kind of mother you deserve
I would have known, I must admit.
But none of us gets that sort of mother.
We're stuck, one and all, with what we have.
Can you forgive me for being human?

Lynn Brookside

DURING A WEEKEND RETREAT I heard Denise describe her despair as the young mother of a very sick baby. Labeled by medical personnel as "at risk," her premature daughter had a birth defect. Although in dire need of nourishment, the infant refused a bottle and cried day and night.

Denise was desperate to stop her shrill cries but could find no way to comfort this tiny person.

After four solid weeks of dealing with this life and death drama, Denise could feel herself buckling under the pressure. She looked down at her screaming baby one day and thought, "I hate you! I hate that you won't eat. I hate the turmoil you've brought into my life. I hate your constant screaming. I hate that you might die." In that moment she felt the urge to throw her baby against the wall to quiet her wails. Fortunately, she called her husband at work instead. He quickly came to her aid and Denise was able to sob out her frustrations within his embrace.

Denise felt appalled at herself. This was the child they had wanted for so long, whom she loved so dearly. What kind of mother was she to feel such hatred for this helpless little one? How could she have come to this place? Never dreaming herself capable of such negative emotions, Denise felt thoroughly ashamed of herself. Once she had admitted her hateful feelings and recognized her breaking point, however, the barrier that separated her from her feelings of love and concern for her baby dissipated.

Denise loved her daughter, but she felt hatred toward her at the same time. Her fear that her daughter might die left her feeling spent and powerless. This young mother needed someone to help her carry the immense responsibility of caring for this fragile life. Confessing her hate and fear to God, seeking assistance from her husband and friends, and getting additional medical support helped to alleviate her helplessness and isolation. Settling her jangled nerves provided the emotional space she needed to maneuver successfully between her feelings of love and hate, to choose to act out of her love for her baby.

During that one horrifying moment, Denise could have chosen to quickly deny and submerge her feelings of hatred. Because she was willing to openly acknowledge them instead, she became able to follow that hate back to its deeper roots —her feelings of fear and helplessness. Knowing the real problem allowed her to take the necessary steps to alleviate the causes for those feelings.

Norma shared a similar story about her teenage daughter, Krista. One night when Krista came home drunk, Norma angrily grabbed her arm and yelled at her for what she had done. "The glare in my eyes and my grasp on her arm told her I hated her at that moment. I hated her for disobeying me. I hated her for the anxious, sleepless nights I had spent. I hated her for lying to me. I hated her self-destructive behavior. Our eyes met and I could see that she was hating me back. I released my grip on her arm and we retreated to our separate bedrooms."

This emotionally-charged encounter surprised both mother and daughter. They each had to face the fact that their anger had turned hateful. In the solitude of her bedroom, this mother realized that her love and hate for her daughter were both real. She felt relieved that Krista was all right, that she had returned home safely. At the same time, Norma felt very angry about the broken trust between them. She recognized the fact that these extreme feelings of love and hate sprang from her fear of losing her daughter.

Krista's hatred was real too. Krista hated being judged. More than that, she hated being disapproved of by someone whose opinion she cared about deeply—someone she loved.

In such volatile moments, we can come eyeball-to-eyeball with one another's hate. Such encounters demonstrate how love sometimes gives rise to hate. Our strongest emotions, including both love and hate, are usually directed toward those about whom we care the most. We don't generally feel tremendous anger with those who mean little to us.

Hatred tends to grow out of unresolved anger. It develops when we are feeling overwhelmed by our anger, fears, and frustrations—the way Denise felt when her tiny baby was so ill. Or it grows out of repeated episodes of "gunny-sacking," when we stuff our anger down inside and don't deal with it until we have a sack full—as Norma did with her daughter. Krista's drunkenness that night was the proverbial straw that broke the camel's back. Norma's anger had lain smoldering within her heart and mind until it turned to hate in one explosive instant.

Like cream in a butter churn, anger with members of our family solidifies into an instant of hatred more often than most of us like to admit. Yet, many of us have difficulty accepting the idea that we can feel that angry with someone we love so very dearly.

MEETING SOMEWHERE IN THE MIDDLE

One six-year-old child expressed it this way: "When Mommy's mad, she talks with a smack in her voice!" Children have not yet learned to revere rationality. Because they do not find ambiguous feelings so bothersome, they may feel quite free to express extremely different emotions in rapid succession. It isn't unusual to hear a child say "I hate you," one moment and "I love you" the next. Perhaps we should learn a lesson from their honesty.

The extent to which children feel anger hit home for me one afternoon when I overheard my six-year-old daughter talking to a seven-year-old who lived nearby. Terribly upset with his father, this boy was spitting out vengeful words like "I hate him! I'd like to kill him!" I was surprised by the force of his feelings and felt sorry for what had transpired between him and his father.

Just as I was about to intervene and help him deal with these hateful feelings, my daughter piped up with, "I know just what you mean. I feel that way about my mother, too. Sometimes I get so mad at her, I'd like to give her a jab in the rear end."

I stepped back in instant humility. My daughter experienced those same intense feelings of anger toward me! In that moment, I had to admit that I had my own angry feelings toward her from time to time, and that they sometimes came out in hateful ways. I flashed back to the week before when I had scolded her with more vehemence than was necessary. Because we become so good at pushing such strong emotions away and pretending they never happened, we can be shocked when we finally admit to their existence.

How can it be that love and hate are so closely connected? We usually picture these emotions at opposite ends of a straight line. When we describe positive and negative feelings toward someone, we mentally put love and hate at different ends of a continuum. But in reality, they are not poles apart. In fact, love and hate circle around, ending up right next to each other. Indeed, these feelings become inextricably intertwined around our deepest relationships.

The confusion that arises from assuming that these emotions are opposites can be corrected by this circular view. It's precisely because we care so deeply about our mothers that we get so angry with them when things go awry. It's *apathy*, rather than *hate*, that is antithetical to love. Anger indicates that our feelings are alive, that we are emotionally invested in the relationship. That's one reason why teenagers sometimes try to grab their parents' attention by acting in unacceptable ways. They seem to be saying, "Love me or hate me, but don't ignore me!"

It was Gaye, the quiet one in a women's sharing group, who got in touch with this truth one day. She began by telling the others that it had ceased to matter that her mother never expressed affection to her when she was a child. Gaye explained, quite rationally, that she had grappled too long with the painful question, "Why didn't she love me?" She had no feelings left anymore; she had hardened herself into believing it didn't matter to her. Then, in the middle of this emotionless declaration, Gaye's voice grew louder as she repeated over and over, "I don't care anymore! I don't CARE anymore! **I DON'T CARE ANYMORE!**"

The quake in her body and the quiver in her voice gave Gaye away. She did care and it did matter! This quiet woman by nature began to express her anger by pounding a pillow, releasing her deep disappointment and pain; angry tears flowed freely. The intensity of Gaye's emotions revealed that she cared very much. She decided to find a way to express the pain of her past so that she and her mother might have the chance to end their cold war. It took courage for her to make that decision, but Gaye had learned that the price of continued denial was far too high.

Hatred and anger come in varying levels of intensity. From time to time, most of us experience the normal intense feelings of dislike toward a person we love. When those feelings are not expressed, however, they can grow into destructive feelings of hate, rage, and revenge. Arranged on a simple graph, the mild end might represent minor irritations or disappointments, the middle indicates more significant anger, and the far end represents extreme anger like rage and vengeance:

Disappointment   Frustration   ANGER   Hate   Rage   Revenge

When we fail to admit our minor frustrations and disappointments, our feelings tend to grow more intense. Denial provides fertile ground where anger can grow. Many of us try to push anger away whenever it rears its ugly head. Not dealing with it immediately, however, only causes anger to fester within us until it becomes harmful and retaliatory.

Some of us have been taught that it's not "Christian" to feel angry, but the Bible seems to indicate that anger is a legitimate emotion that we're going to feel from time to time. Ephesians 4:26 says, "Be angry but do not sin; do not let the sun go down on your anger" (RSV). We are cautioned to handle our anger in constructive ways.

When we refrain from expressing anger, we maintain the illusion of keeping our lives neater. Expressing anger can upset things in our lives and force us to live with some ragged edges for a while. Also, we may believe that people will dislike us if we show our anger, that "nice" people don't get angry, that it's not "lady-like" to show anger. When we think about it, however, we can readily see that even "ladies" are members of the human race. All humans feel anger at times.

On the whole, women strive to create community or to connect. Many of us view anger as divisive. We often feel that admitting our anger will weaken our shared bond, whether our community is composed of the mother-daughter dyad or a larger grouping. In that case, we will have defeated our primary task, which is to strengthen community.[1] Nothing could be farther from the truth.

Women often get the impression that the mother-daughter relationship is only to be sweet, mutually nurturing, and loving. Such an idealized view makes it particularly difficult for mothers and daughters to even admit their anger, let alone work it out. So the angry feelings burrow underground. Or if not suppressed and controlled, they are expressed in passively hostile ways or in sideways anger toward innocent bystanders.

Women need to learn to regard anger more objectively. Anger is an emotional signal that tells us things are going wrong. We may be feeling threatened or invalidated. Or we may be feeling abandoned or powerless. Whatever its root, our anger serves as a bright flare that can lead us to what's gone wrong.

When our anger is seen as a *marker* rather than a *threat*, it can spur us to search for solutions. The knowledge we gain by finding those answers will strengthen our communion rather than weaken it. When mothers and daughters face the anger between them, dealing openly and constructively with it, it can not only strengthen their connection but enable them to grow in unforeseen ways.

THE PAY-LATER PLAN

Those of us who keep our anger hidden from our mothers often do so because we fear losing their love. Others may keep it hidden because we fear what we may do if we ever give vent to our anger. We believe that expressing it will unleash disaster, that we will become rejecting, critical, demanding, and guilt-inducing. One woman confessed, "Once I show my anger, I'm afraid I will get so vicious I won't be able to stop. I'll destroy my mother with my anger."

Such a fear acknowledges the fact that anger *is* a powerful emotion. Bloody images can flash through our minds of our anger exploding with such force that it will maim or destroy someone. We fear that it will erupt like a volcano, spewing molten rock from the core of internal pressure built up over many years.

Sensitive to the slightest relationship-tremors, many of us carefully guard against such explosions. The aftermath of emotional fissures is too disruptive. But we suppress our anger at the cost of increasing our internal pressure. We churn now and pay later. Eventually, we can no longer keep the volcano capped. And the longer we keep the lid on, the greater the destruction is likely to be when it finally blows.

Unfortunately, this pay-later plan never gives us the chance to learn to express our anger in appropriate ways before internal pressure builds to gigantic proportions. Anger seeks expression just as surely as night follows day. When it goes underground this powerful emotion often finds expression through physical disorders such as temporomandibular joint pain (TMJ), migraines, ulcers, insomnia, or myriad other symptoms. We may suffer burn-out in our workplace or in our family responsibilities. Or we may resort to "side-ways anger," taking our anger out on an innocent bystander.

The only way to do away with anger is to acknowledge and deal with it. Otherwise it becomes a destructive force, either turned inward or outward. And most of us are more prone to self-destruct rather than risk damaging relationships by expressing our anger in more volatile ways.

Lynea lives within thirty miles of her mother's home, but hasn't spoken to her for twenty years. It all started with insignificant differences. Believing she "shouldn't" be angry with someone she loved, Lynea held her anger in check and never discussed her disagreements with her mother and how they made her feel. Their differences went unresolved and eventually escalated into a full blown battle, ending in a complete stand-off.

Lynea is saddened by the fact that she can't share with her mother the birth of her new child, the accomplishments of her children, or her career successes. The breach between this daughter and her mother is so vast that both continue to live as if the other doesn't even exist—exacting a constant and ongoing toll on everyone concerned. In an effort to "be nice" Lynea has subscribed to the pay-later plan. But she and her mother keep paying... and paying... and paying.

WHAT HAPPENED TO YOUR MAGIC WAND?

A child often grows up believing that mother is all-knowing and all-powerful. Mom seems to know what her child is thinking and even has eyes in the back of her head. We expect our mothers to be there when we need them.

One woman named Cathy told some of her friends that she and her siblings once drew straws to see who would sneak up behind their mother and part the hair at the back of her head. They wanted to get a look at the eyes they were sure they would find there. She laughed as she described the incident, but it was clear that they had been completely serious about it at the time.

Cathy is still having difficulty forgiving her mother—who claims that she didn't know that Cathy was being sexually abused in her own home. Because as a little girl she really believed that her mother was all-knowing, Cathy finds it difficult to believe, even now, that her mother wasn't deliberately ignoring her need for safety and protection.

Children accept motherly guidance, believing they know everything there is to know about everything. We actively seek her approval and help. As youngsters, we don't really want to believe our mothers make mistakes, even though we grapple with the fact that they are very human. Eventually we learn that "even mothers make mistakes," as Judith Viorst's delightful children's book tells us.[2] As we grow older we begin to question this all-knowing concept of our mothers. And in adolescence we question almost everything they do or say.

Individuation—the development of our own completely separate identity—usually involves rebellion, whether that rebellion is open or surreptitious. During our teenage years ferocious battles can be waged over minor issues like food, clothes, friends, activities, school, and work. You name it, and we'll disagree about it. We seem to know intuitively how to get under our parents' skin as we begin to spread our wings. This power struggle can wreak all kinds of havoc in our relationships.

Some mothers and teenage daughters fight like cats, snarling and scratching at each other. Some prefer to stand at a distance and launch verbal strikes which are equally hurtful. Some are more subtle, using silent put downs that are, nevertheless, potent elements in a power struggle. Adolescent anger may give a daughter the excuse she's been seeking to develop an identity separate from her mother's—which is an essential part of growth and health.

These turbulent years often hit a mother at a particularly vulnerable time in her own life cycle. She may herself be going through some sort of mid-life crisis just as her daughter is beginning to blossom. The contrasts tend to accentuate their differences. Mother may be asking herself, "Is this all there is to life?" while daughter may be looking forward to all the sweet possibilities of the future. When they walk down the street together, men may notice the daughter rather than the mother. When daughter tells mother to hold her stomach in, mother confesses that she *is* holding it in. Such sexually laden identity issues make this a particularly sensitive time for both mother and daughter.

Daughters may feel they should not compete with their mothers. Or they may worry about what would happen if they do become more successful than their mothers. Most teenaged daughters wonder—either consciously or unconsciously—whether their desire to separate from their mothers expresses disloyalty.

This time of separation can be very scary for both mothers and daughters. It's no wonder that anger often grows out of our gut-wrenching fear. Even as teenagers, most of us retain somewhere deep within part of that little girl belief in her all-powerful mother. Daughters can't always help feeling angry when Mother doesn't wave her magic wand and make the "scare" go away. But she can't. And we can't. It's something we must simply live through.

And when we become adults, we must forgive each other for whatever mistakes we may have made along the tortuous way. What are some of the more common mothering styles that can throw up roadblocks in our paths?

The controlling mother. Florence Nightingale, the heroic founder of modern nursing, once wrote these despairing words, "I have so long been a child!" A turbulent relationship with her controlling mother nearly cost her sanity.[3] When a daughter can't seem to separate from her mother, a sense of hopelessness sets in. Anger is often born of hopelessness. Controlling mothers often hover over their daughters like birds of prey, making it extremely difficult for their daughters to separate from them without feeling disloyal or guilty.

On the opposite extreme, some mothers focus so intently on their own problems that they separate themselves from their daughters far too early. Daughters in this situation feel hopeless because they can't change the problems their mothers face. Once again, anger is born of this hopelessness.

To complicate matters, this daughter can't even express her anger to her mother because Mother is unavailable to listen. She's too involved with her own problems—whether it's a narcissistic self-focus, her own ill health, the ill health of a family member, emotional problems, or the crushing responsibility of raising her children alone. Whatever difficulties cause a mother to separate from her daughter too soon, you can be sure that the daughter will feel the emotional abandonment keenly. And whether hopelessness grows from too little or too much separation, anger is usually the bottom line.

The alcoholic mother. Huddled together in Sonia's living room, a group of adult daughters of alcoholic mothers watched the video, *Postcards from the Edge.* They each groaned, laughed, cried, and ached as the all too familiar scenes flashed before them on the screen. The long-sealed vaults where they had stored up years of old anger toward their detached, narcissist mothers began to open.

Comparing their lives with friends who had a "normal" mother-daughter relationship made them even more aware of their deprivation. Indeed, these women had missed out on something every girl is supposed to enjoy: a close relationship with her mother. The movie reminded them that something had been missing for them as they had moved toward adulthood. These friends grew more sober as the movie came to a close and they began to process their emotional reactions.

Two women felt only numbness toward their mothers. They expressed the overwhelming loneliness of this alienation. Betty remarked, "It's better to feel nothing. When you're emotionally dead you're protected from the rage that comes of being powerless. My powerlessness has crushed me down and I can't get up enough courage to fight anymore."

Three women expressed extreme anger, claiming special hardship because the mother is *supposed* to be the emotional caretaker. When their mothers didn't fulfill that role, each of them believed there was something wrong with *them*, not their mothers. Each one asked, "Why wasn't I enough reason for her to stop drinking?" They lived with denial so long— pretending things were normal when they were abnormal— that they were finally unsure of reality at all. They all felt rage at the messages they had received as children: DON'T FEEL. DON'T TALK. DON'T TRUST. They described an ache in their soul that follows them everywhere and never goes away.

Janice listened to her mother's heartache for most of her life. She stood by helplessly, watching her mother use alcohol as a solution to her problems. This growing girl felt guilty for not being able to fix her mother's problems. Worse still, she never felt free to share her own problems, which seemed insignificant in contrast to her mother's crises. Her mother always seemed out of it, focusing on her next drink, planning ways to fool the family, hiding the truth from herself and others, raging at her husband, blacking out. Janice ended her anguished outpouring: "The truth is, I didn't have a mother."

The hearts of her friends ache for her... and for themselves. Life was unpredictable and unstable for all of these women. They could never count on their mothers to be there for the special events in their lives. And when they did show up, they usually embarrassed their daughters.

Betty protected herself from the hurt by becoming more and more withdrawn from friends. Sonia never learned how to be in a relationship with her mother without giving up her own life. She could find no way to separate from a mother who needed her so desperately and would not let go. Sonia's world had become so focused on her mother's alcoholism that she had no life of her own. Booze had pulled her into a battle she couldn't win.

These women finally found help through the Al-Anon program. For the first time, they began to realize that they could do something for themselves, even though they could not save their mothers. Listening to others describe similar struggles within their own alcoholic families helped these women to know that they weren't alone. They found support as they began to detach from their mothers and forge a life for themselves. As they changed their own behavior they gained new hope for their own future and for their future mother-daughter relationship.

The abusive mother. When a daughter has been abused, physically or sexually or emotionally, by her mother, it leaves a kind of rage that is not easily resolved. Lewis Smedes describes why this betrayal is so devastating: "Hate within our circle of committed love is the most virulent kind. It does not affect us so much when we hate a person who never promised to be with us, never walked with us on our private paths, never played the strings of our soul. But when a person destroys what our commitment and our intimacy created, something precious is destroyed. Hate for people we love makes us sick."[4]

A daughter trusts that she will be safe in a circle of love with her mother. Her sense of betrayal runs deep when this trust is broken. Living in the midst of this emotional turmoil, a child tends to turn her hate inward, further destroying herself. It's too scary to hate Mommy, the person she looks to not only for safety but for the necessities of life. In a child's eyes, it's safer to turn anger inward than risk abandonment.

That's how it was for Tonia, who was physically and sexually abused by her mother. She wrote the following letter to me when I asked my friend for her thoughts on anger toward one's mother.

My Dear Friend,

The hardest thing about anger towards Mother is giving oneself permission to feel it and then, of course, the leap of courage to express it. Usually some empowering person has to give us permission—sometimes a wise friend, more often a therapist or pastoral counselor. In my many years in therapy I have seen many a person sacrifice her wholeness on The Altar of Mama rather than admit that anything was wrong with Mother.

I'm sure I'm biased but... [I believe] that the most difficult mothers are those who will say and do whatever is necessary to look good to the outside world, regardless of what sickness occurs within the family's walls. A *lie* is lived... [for the sake of] appearance-management and Mother trains her children to swallow their anger.

For me, I stopped swallowing it when I was thirteen. I crossed the line and called my mother a bitch to her face. There was no one in my world to give me permission to be angry and guide me to use my anger for good. So I trod down the path of a vile-mouthed teenager and as soon as I left home I rebelled against everything I had been taught. Good and holy standards were chucked out of the window along with appearance-management standards. I had [learned] no discernment to distinguish between the two.

I didn't know how to use anger and I didn't know how to feel it without guilt. The longer I was away from home the guiltier I felt because the memories of her duplicity grew dimmer as I lived out on my own. When I became a Christian this guilt was magnified because I was sure I needed to forgive whatever it was that I was angry about. I did this to the best of my ability, but generic forgiveness of nameless sins is a fairly powerless experience.

I believe God peeled away the layers of my anger gradually. First he exposed my deep longings for my mother's affection and touch. My mother was a cold woman within our walls, although warm and funny to outsiders. I never once remember being touched or kissed. In a very painful dream I realized that my mother was a physical mother only and that she would never be an emotional mother. That anger and expectation of [receiving] something from her had to be laid aside.

I continued to live my life with serious bouts of depression where I functioned like a mindless robot. It was anger turned inward. My mother had controlled and manipulated every activity; she had literally tried to take over my thoughts and feelings. There was no dealing with anger on her territory. She frightened me to my bones! It was only when I moved five hundred miles away that I could begin to deal successfully with my mother-rage. My fear level and depth of rage were intricately knit together based on my fear of losing her love if I expressed my anger.

In the safety... [provided by] that distance I began my long recovery process. I finally realized how my mother's opinions had taken me over. She had run roughshod over me so I nicknamed her "thought police." When I could giggle inside with this label I could keep from getting drawn into the old messages and debates between myself and her voice within me.

Awareness is more than three-quarters of the battle. Once my mother called unexpectedly and went into one of her verbal... tirades. I was reduced to a blithering idiot and felt like a helpless child. It triggered all the childhood memories. This opened up the horrible abuse that I had suffered as a child and I ended up having a complete mental breakdown. The eleven weeks I spent in a mental hospital was the first time I began to confront the horrible memories of my physical and sexual abuse as a child.

Even with medication and daily therapy I could only deal with the anger a teaspoon at a time. I was a prisoner of my anger, but the expression of truth... allowed me to let go of subconscious expectations for nurture, protection, and love from my mother.

I still deal quite painfully with my mother's legacy... of self-hatred and total sexual confusion. Sometimes I wish I could exact some kind of payment because it costs me so much in time and energy to pursue recovery. But anger rests [because] I know her to be a prisoner of the evil one—sold out to a lie that she's done the best she can. In a way, that's true, but that only makes it more pathetic.

I look to God for my nurture and protection and love, and he sends it in worship with his people.

Well, that's what poured out as I ruminated on anger. It was a helpful exercise for me; hope it's helpful to your readers.

Tonia

HEALING THE HATE

We have examined how we can hate the same person we love—or used to love. And we have seen that a flash of hatred is an unfortunate but predictable outgrowth of accumulated anger, anger born of overwhelming fears and frustrations. But we must not confuse the sort of hate that flashes through us temporarily and the sort of hate that can become a constant in our lives. And we must never confuse anger with such long-lasting hatred. Lewis Smedes speaks to this important distinction:

> It is hate and not anger that needs healing. Anger is a sign that we are alive and well. Hate is a sign that we are sick and need to be healed. Healthy anger drives us to do something to change what makes us angry; anger can

energize us to make things better. Hate does not want to change things for the better; it wants to make things worse. Hate wants to belch the foul breath of death over a life that love alone creates.[5]

When we *entertain* hatred—when we invite it to pull up a chair and make itself at home—we do indeed allow it to belch the foul breath of death over our lives. If you were abused and neglected as a child, you'll never forget it because no atrocity can ever really be forgotten. Yet healing can bring freedom from hatred when we let God take the vengeance out of our soul.

My friend, Tonia, a woman who has been on this journey for many years, salutes the community of loving healers who have given her the ability to forgive and let go. She has discovered, along with numerous others like her, that we can fearlessly traverse the circle that connects hate and love and find healing along the way.

Our own differences with our mothers probably haven't affected our lives as profoundly as Tonia's life was affected by her cruel and abusive mother. Even so, ignoring our anger will eventually—far from creating connection—separate and destroy, manifesting itself in aggressive acts against others or against ourselves. But when we pay attention to our anger, we can right the wrongs in our relationships. We can seek solutions and avail ourselves of God's healing power. Before we go on to consider specific ways of dealing with mother-daughter anger, take some time to consider how anger has surfaced in your own life.

Exercises

1. Think of a time when you felt very angry toward your mother as a child. How old were you and what led to your

angry feelings? What did you do to show your anger? How did your mother respond?

2. Now ask yourself what you *wish* had happened in that same situation? How would you have liked your mother to respond to your expression of anger? What difference would this have made for you?

3. Write down all the words you use to express your anger. Now place these statements on a graph, with mild at one end, severe at the other, and anger right in the middle. At what end of the continuum did you have the most words? Do you ever have feelings that fall under the headings rage, hate, revenge—even though you may not voice them? How do you feel about yourself as you reflect on your anger?

4. What do you think Ephesians 4:26 means by the admonishment to "not let the sun go down on your anger"? What principles does this verse address? Just as inappropriately expressed anger can lead to actual harm, even mild forms of anger held over a long time can have a devastating effect on you and on others. Can you name any examples of this truth in your relationship with your mother?

5. Try to remember a time when you were angry, first as a little girl, then as a teenager, and finally as an adult woman. What caused you to feel such anger? How did you handle your anger? How was your anger greeted by family members? What noticeable patterns can you see, like anger repeatedly springing from the same unmet need or desire?

6. Write down on a piece of paper a time as an adult woman when you were angry at your mother:

I was angry when _____

_____.

What I did was _____

_____.

What my mother did was _____

_____.

What my body did was _____

_____.

What I would like to have done was _____

_____.

Take time to evaluate these responses. How can you follow through by actually expressing your anger to your mother in a constructive way?

7. If you lived in a home where dysfunction or abuse took place, how have you dealt with the legitimate anger you feel about that situation? Have you distinguished between anger and hate? Write down three specific things you can do to work toward healing.

EIGHT

Conflict:
How We Hate It!

Authentic love is a dance with three movements: solo, counter-
point, and coming together; it embraces solitude, conflict, and
intimacy. Leave any one of the three movements out and you
destroy the dance.   Sam Keen

L OVE AND CONFLICT GO TOGETHER. In his book, *Fire in the*
Belly, Sam Keen implies that conflict is in fact the *pivotal*
movement in the dance of love, the essential step that carries
two people to a point of intimacy.[1] When we form an identity
separate from that of our mothers (solo), the expression of
our own thoughts, feelings, and ideas inevitably produces
conflict (counterpoint). Speaking for ourselves in a respectful way can then lead to increased understanding and intimacy between us.

A relationship requires two people. As long as mother and

daughter try to function as a single unit, their relationship will be strained. A daughter needs to separate enough to express her true feelings and pronounce a clear no to her mother. Two-year-olds usually pull this off with gusto. Yet the same child will also be able to say a clear yes when she wishes. As in an intricate dance, daughters are free to *connect* with their mothers only when they are truly *separate* from them.

If we believe that love equals complete unity, anger leaves us feeling disturbed. In truth, love evokes conflict. Two people who care deeply for one another will invariably grate on each other's nerves, sooner or later. When the point of conflict is handled openly—with an eye to finding solutions rather than blaming—the resolution produces greater intimacy and harmony, rubbing our rough edges smooth. We learn more about ourselves in the process, which benefits us and all those with whom we have relationships.

Conflict within our mother-daughter relationships can afford us an opportunity to express ourselves as equals. Like most women, you may tend to seek intimacy through connection, which implies equality. Men more typically strive for unequal status through power plays and the like. When given the proper tools, women are naturally motivated to turn conflict into a chance to understand one another better.[2]

CONNECTING THROUGH CONFLICT

One of the tools that can assist us in that effort is learning more about the various ways of dealing with conflict. In their book entitled *Interpersonal Conflict,* Joyce Hocker and William Wilmot identify five standard conflict styles: the yielder; the winner; the negotiator; the withdrawer; and the pursuer.[3] Let's explore these different approaches with an eye toward learning more about handling disagreements more graciously. In particular, try to picture your typical interactions with your mother.

The yielder. The conflict style used by many women is that of the yielder. If you are a yielder, you placate and give in to others. You give and give and give some more. You usually don't speak out or talk back. You often don't have opinions about what to do or where to go; if you do, you hesitate to express them. You let others make decisions for you. You are the one who serves their needs.

The yielder may feel angry inside, but rarely expresses it verbally. Anger sometimes gets expressed in passive-aggressive ways, like being particularly slow, or habitually late, or "forgetting" things that are important to others. You may use illness or some other legitimate excuses to say no, but seldom assert a choice that appears to be for your own sake.

One former yielder said it took her years to own her anger, but when she did it was the most empowering experience of her life. She felt incredibly free in no longer feeling the need to placate others. However, this freedom was also very frightening for her. Having and expressing opinions can be very scary business. It seemed safer not to pursue her own needs or wants, when she didn't feel responsible if things went wrong.

Those who live with placaters often feel angry with them; they feel guilty for "taking advantage" of them. Yielding can actually become a position of power as others invest themselves in trying to guess how to please the yielder. This, too, gives rise to anger because there are so many chances to guess wrongly.

For example, a yielder-mother may tell her adult daughter that she doesn't care where they go to eat, even while she secretly hopes her daughter will choose her preferred place. Then after they have finished eating in the restaurant of her daughter's choosing, the yielder-mother may make a comment like, "I guess you didn't remember I'm allergic to MSG so there was very little I could order from the menu, but I'm glad *you* enjoyed the food." Such a remark leaves the daughter feeling bad and manipulated. Since it's too late to change her choice, she naturally feels angry that her mother didn't express herself when she had the chance.

The winner. Winners invest themselves in winning. If you're a winner, you may be extremely successful both at work and at home. Having developed strong verbal skills, you're accustomed to convincing others of the validity of your ideas. You use forceful, logical arguments to get your way. If you use the winner style in dealing with conflict, you probably find friendly debate—what others might call arguing—to be exhilarating. You love it when you finally win your point. And you usually truly believe you have the best solution to a problem.

A mother who is a winner may be described as "proud" and tends to treat her daughter as an underling. She makes most of the decisions and takes charge of the relationship. She usually gets her way, but may lose her relationship with her daughter in the process. In the same lunch scene, a winner-mother easily convinces her daughter where they should meet for lunch, but her daughter may arrive feeling disgruntled because her desires were hardly considered. They will probably have a strained lunch, enjoying neither the food or conversation.

The negotiator. Compromise is the key word for the negotiator. If you're a negotiator, you enjoy seeing everyone get something in the end. You listen to all sides of the story, all opinions, as well as openly expressing your own viewpoint. You value the democratic process since it gives everyone an equal chance to express their opinions. You like decisions to be based on majority-rule so that, presumably, the greatest number of people will be satisfied.

Since negotiators like everyone to be happy, you may play the role of peacemaker in a group, directing conversation so everyone understands the other points of view. You have a great sense of fairness and see collaboration as the most productive way to make decisions. Because you want everyone to have an equal opportunity to be heard, reaching a decision may take awhile.

As a negotiator, you're willing to be influenced by others and happily tolerate disparate opinions. Even though you have your own convictions, you change willingly when you see validity in another person's arguments. Sometimes this negotiability makes it difficult for you to take a firm position and stick to it. Some might call you wishy-washy or criticize you for giving in too soon for the sake of peace.

The biggest drawback in dealing with a negotiator is that nobody gets exactly what she wants when compromise is the order of the day. A negotiator-mother may spend an inordinate amount of time deciding where to go for lunch. Since she and her daughter have different opinions, they may decide on a neutral place that's really no one's first choice. In this scenario, both of them must give up what they really want for the sake of compromise.

The withdrawer. Withdrawers don't like conflict of any kind. If you're a withdrawer, you feel safer physically or emotionally leaving the scene of conflict rather than facing it directly. You try not to become emotionally involved in issues so that it's easier to extricate yourself when a dispute arises.

Women who habitually use this mode of dealing with conflict frequently grew up in a dysfunctional family. You learned to withdraw for the sake of survival, perhaps using it to avoid physical or emotional harm. When caught in the midst of a conflict, you hope that it will eventually resolve itself and people's anger will dissipate without your participation.

If you're a withdrawer, you learn to push your negative feelings away. Or you relieve the tension through other means, like physical activity, rather than through direct confrontation. You tend to be a great escape artist and it takes effort to pin you down. A withdrawer must be given space and time to think in order to deal with conflict. You will find it difficult to deal with the conflict on the spot and, if pushed, will simply become overwhelmed and leave the scene anyway. Frequently, you will need to retreat from the intensity of the conflict in order to sort out your thoughts and feelings. Only then will you be willing to interact over the conflict. But, it will still be a struggle from which you'll flee if things get too intense.

The withdrawer-mother tends to make decisions on her own, without consulting her daughter about them. She often views the world as basically unsafe and plans her life accordingly. This mother may be a loner and, if you want to go out to eat, you go where she has already planned to go. If you suggest a restaurant that isn't to her liking, the withdrawer-mother may go along without openly protesting. But she may be knocked off kilter and will tend to feel terribly uncomfortable, invariably finding something wrong with the place or the food.

Daughters of withdrawers tend to give in and do it mother's way in order to have a relationship with her. But, of course, the daughter will frequently become resentful if she must continually capitulate in order to be with her mother.

The pursuer. Pursuers are idealistic. If you're a pursuer, you believe a perfect solution exists to every problem, one in which everyone's needs will be met. Compromise is not an option, because that means someone doesn't get what she wants. You tend to be intense and persistent, needing to solve conflicts because disruption in the relationship cannot be tolerated. You typically can't rest until you find a solution, and it's difficult for you to get on with the rest of your life when a conflict is on hold.

The pursuer-mother will tend to invest a lot in her relationship with her daughter. Intent on developing it to a maximum degree, she keeps working at it throughout life. In choosing a place to eat, the pursuer-mother won't stop until she finds just the right place that suits both *her* fancy as well as her *daughter's*. If her daughter expresses discontent, this mother will continue to pursue every alternative until mutual satisfaction is assured. The daughter may want to drop the idealism and just make a decision, but it will be difficult for the pursuer to settle for anything less than the ideal.

MESHING CONFLICT STYLES

No one style is better than the others. As you can see from the descriptions above, each one tends to offer certain advantages and disadvantages. Every person uses a predominant style in their interactions. Your style is the most natural way for you to deal with personal conflict. You probably learned your particular style because it worked best for you within your family of origin and because it suited your personality.

Other members of your family will often adopt a different style because it suits their own temperament and the role they play within your family system. In considering your mother-daughter relationship, it's important for you to identify the styles which you and your mother use in dealing with the conflicts that arise between you.

Some combinations are more common than others. Why might this happen? One reason may be that when a mother has a particular style, that fact tends to engender an *opposite* style in her daughter. For instance, when a mother is a pursuer, her daughter tends to adopt the style of a withdrawer. If a pursuer has two daughters, however, then one of them may adopt a *third* style because she perceives that her sister has already "taken" the role of the withdrawer. In such a case, a second (or third, etc.) daughter might adopt the style of a winner, particularly if she happens to be more extraverted.

So many factors figure into what role a person may assume that it would be impossible to cover every possible combination. Here are three examples of the more common ones to help you analyze your own combination of conflict styles. Once you understand your interpersonal dynamics better, you will be better equipped to work toward smoother conflict resolution.

Of course, not every mother and daughter are both *willing* to improve this key area of their relationship. You may need to assume an active role in *asking* to be heard or in finding new ways of dealing with confrontation. Remember, when one person changes the dance steps, the partner must learn a new way of responding.

Winner/winner. If you and your mother are both winners, you can expect a lot of fireworks. You will have strong verbal battles in which you may find it particularly hard to listen to one another because you're both busy arguing your case. You may or may not enjoy the interaction. It can easily become a power struggle and you may be uncomfortably aware of the fact that someone has to win.

On the other hand, you may each leave the scene believing you've won, even when you haven't really resolved anything at all. You both manage the impasse by convincing yourselves that you've won your point. But it's also possible for your battles to become so heated that you both feel defeated in the end, in which case nobody is a winner. Or perhaps one of you consistently wins, which leaves the other winner feeling totally outmaneuvered and harms the relationship in the process.

When two winners wish to maintain a healthy relationship, they find it best to set certain ground rules, agreeing not to sacrifice their love in their urgency to win the daily skirmishes. You may need to arrange to take turns during a heated discussion, deciding that one of you will speak while the other listens silently. To make sure you've understood one another, you could agree to reflect back what you feel you've heard and respond accordingly. After listening to one another, both of you could also try to verbalize strengths in the opposing viewpoint. The ideas you agree upon could then be used to formulate a united position.

If setting these kinds of ground rules seems impossible, you may want to agree that you can both be winners even when you come up with different solutions. In other words, agree to disagree! Being a winner doesn't always have to mean wiping out the enemy. As you try to gain appreciation for the other's point of view, that could become an even greater victory worth celebrating.

Pursuer/withdrawer. In this dyad, one will naturally pursue and the other will naturally seek to distance, which can eventually lead to a breakdown in the relationship. If your mother is the pursuer, you as a withdrawer will find creative ways to rebuff her approaches while keeping personal insights and thoughts to yourself.

Feeling locked out will frustrate the pursuer-mother who wants a close relationship and needs to have issues settled. Her emotional energy will increase when disagreements are not resolved. You as a withdrawer will continue to seek distance because you feel engulfed and overwhelmed by your mother's intensity. This dance generally continues until one of you blows up, creating more alienation.

In this interaction of styles, you could recommend that your mother try to be more patient. Ask her to allow you enough space and time to think things through before talking it out. You will need enough strength and self-respect to state your case without worrying that your pursuer-mother will out-talk or out-maneuver you. Because you fear your mother's intensity, you may tend to back down in her presence, even when you don't really agree. You may simply want to get your mother to back off. Even though you know this is a false resolution, you may not see any other way out.

In forging a new style for resolving conflicts, you will need to resist this natural tendency. Agree to spend some time away from your mother to think about the conflict instead of just escaping from it. Writing down your thoughts may help you to express yourself more clearly when you do meet again. Both of you could decide on a time to come back together to deal with the issue.

During this meeting, ask your mother to let you talk first without interruption. Take as much time as you need to clearly and non-defensively communicate your viewpoint, using written notes if helpful. Ask your mother just to listen and try to understand your position. After you've finished, you may suggest that your mother keep herself to a reasonable time limit. Because if she talks too long or if things become too intense, you may simply withdraw—emotionally if not physically.

Once both of you have had an opportunity to state your case, it may be helpful to take time to process and clarify what each of you has said. A fifteen-minute break may help you as a withdrawer to gather your thoughts. Then when you come together again, you can try to find a solution acceptable to both of you. Your mother must give up her unrelenting pursuit of the ideal; you must give up the idea that avoidance solves conflicts.

Negotiator/yielder. If your mother is a negotiator and you are a yielder, it is very important for you to express your opinion. Your mother may want you to say more than you feel comfortable saying. Often, you aren't even in touch with your own needs, so expressing yourself may be more difficult than either of you imagines.

In trying to draw you out, your mother can appear patronizing if she's not careful. You may be inclined to go along with her, just because she does have clear opinions. Listening will usually be a lot easier than expressing your own desires. You may even have built up resentments over the years that will need to be cleared up before a more positive interaction can take place.

It will be important to arrange a comfortable environment in which you feel encouraged, but not pressured, to talk. Request a respectful encounter in which you can express yourself freely without any prodding or interruptions from your mother. Ask her to let you speak first and to patiently hear you out. Written notes may be helpful. Then ask your mother to express her thoughts and ideas as statements of preference, without trying to convince or persuade. Ask each other questions to clarify any statements you don't fully understand.

It may take time to reach a final decision on which you can both agree. When your differences can't be resolved, perhaps you could take turns choosing a solution. You may need more experience in making choices for yourself while still respecting your mother's need for fairness.

HOW DO WE DEAL WITH ANGER?

Obviously, many more combinations exist, but each mother-daughter dyad needs to work out their own system for dealing with conflict and the resultant anger. There are four basic ways of dealing with anger:

YOU CAN EXPRESS IT!
YOU CAN SUPPRESS IT!
YOU CAN REPRESS IT!
YOU CAN CONFESS IT!

Expressing anger. You can express anger in many ways. You can do it indirectly by letting it seep into all of your actions in numerous tiny ways, or you can express it directly. But even the direct approach requires a choice. You can choose to make your expression of anger either constructive or destructive. You can be physically or verbally abusive, or you can find a way to assert yourself without being abusive.

Being *assertive* means maintaining self-control. You refrain from belittling or blaming. You express yourself in a concise and direct manner. This approach leaves your self-esteem unharmed because you haven't violated your own ethical framework. You're able to get angry and still face yourself in the morning. You no longer need to hide your anger from your mother once you've learned how to express it in a way that acknowledges her integrity and her right to differ with you.

In learning how to express your anger assertively, you may find it helpful to practice with a trusted friend who can give you feedback about how you come across. This kind of dry-run can also provide you an opportunity to vent some of your feelings beforehand, thereby defusing some of the angry energy that might otherwise become destructive. Practice will enable you to assert yourself in a forthright, constructive manner.

Suppressing anger. When you suppress your anger, you're *aware* of your feelings but have consciously decided not to express them directly for a number of reasons. Your mother may be out of touch for a while, providing no opportunity to confront your differences with her in a timely fashion. She may be ill, in which case you may need to wait until she is feeling better. If she has recently experienced some personal difficulty, loss, or disappointment, you might want to give her some time before you bring up an area of conflict.

If you decide to suppress your anger for a time, you will need to find a substitute way to release that energy. Methods may include walking or jogging, playing tennis, kneading bread, scrubbing floors, or some other physical activity. Some people find it helpful to tear paper or pound on a pillow as they verbally release their pent up angry feelings.

When you suppress your anger, you are choosing not to deal with it in its purest form by confronting the specific issue that prompted your anger. Rather, you are consciously deciding to "bleed off" your angry energy in physical ways so that you won't recycle that energy in destructive ways within your body or within your other relationships.

Repressing anger. Repression is a form of *denial*, a way of dealing with anger which is never helpful. However, this automatic, *unconscious* reaction often kicks in because we've been taught that anger isn't "okay." We learn to swallow our anger as a sort of knee-jerk reaction because we've learned to fear being angry.

You may fear your anger because of the misperception that being angry isn't "Christian." Or you may have grown up in a home where an adult expressed his or her anger in a destructive way and you don't want to be like that person. Whatever the reason for repressing it, the anger doesn't simply vanish into thin air. It's simply stored somewhere in your body, poisoning your heart and mind. Turning your anger on yourself won't help either you or your mother and will inevitably take its toll in physical or emotional disorders.

Giving yourself *permission* to feel your anger helps you to become aware of angry feelings before you automatically repress them. You need to acknowledge that anger is not damaging in itself and is often a perfectly sane, appropriate response to a given situation. It's what you *do* with your anger that can be destructive and you do have control over that decision. When you feel competent to express your anger in a loving, assertive way, you won't be as tempted to repress anger when you feel it.

Confessing Anger. Confessing anger is another option which is closely related to expressing anger. Expression allows us to vent our angry energy, whether to our mothers or to an objective third party. Confession can help to open the door for discussion as well.

You may want to confess your anger to God or to another person as a way to acknowledge your feelings and get them out into the open. Confession can impart perspective by putting you in a better position to evaluate the reason behind the anger. After rationally examining the basis for your anger, you can decide just what you need to do about it.

While I was on the phone with my mother some time ago, I confessed that I was angry with her for not spending the holidays with me. My father doesn't travel well because of severe arthritis and had asked her to stay home with him. I felt that I deserved some of her time as well. But in the course of the discussion that ensued, I also realized I was angry because she wouldn't stand up to my father and choose to be with me. When I could acknowledge my anger and the desire behind it, we could deal more openly and honestly with the conflict between us rather than trying to pick up hidden messages over the phone.

My confession drew us closer and helped us explore alternatives. Mother was glad to know I wanted to be with her. She expressed her desire to be with me as well, yet decided to stay home anyway for her own reasons. Once she had listened openly to my feelings, I could respect Mom's decision. We arranged for her to visit another time so that my father wouldn't have to be alone during the holidays—a reasonable compromise to our impasse.

Confession of anger may include asking for forgiveness. I recently expressed anger toward my daughter about her dishonesty, but I also confessed sorrow that my judgmental attitude had contributed to her fear of telling me the truth. Asking her forgiveness cleared the air between us. I reaffirmed my commitment to be less critical and judgmental so she would be more willing to be honest with me. My confession gave us an opportunity to deal with past mistakes and bridged the way to a new future.

BUILDING BRIDGES OUT OF ANGER

Awareness is a key word in any discussion of anger. We need to *identify* our angry feelings while they're still on the mild end of the anger graph and *embrace* them as important messages that help us deal with our relationships. We need to ask ourselves what's irritating us or what triggered that sharp tone of voice. What's behind the irritation we feel?

Irritation may stem from the perception that we're not being listened to or understood, that we're not being treated fairly or respected, that we're being rejected or judged defective, or any number of other deep concerns. Whatever the reason, once we are aware of the anger and what's behind it, we have an opportunity to work toward change.

Of course we won't necessarily get the changes we want. But we can feel good about the fact that we were willing to take a risk when we asked that our feelings be addressed and respected. Taking responsibility for our anger—whether in our mother-daughter relationship or another relationship—can be very healthy.

Here is a simple formula for constructive expression of anger:

1. Remember to give an invitation and a "stroke" before you express your anger. A simple statement such as, "Mother, you're probably not aware of this but I'm angry with you. You're so helpful to others all the time, I know you're busy, but I'd like to talk with you about it. Is this a good time?"

2. Express yourself in a non-blaming way without making demands and take full responsibility for your angry feelings. Be precise, concise, and direct by using the following formula (no more than ten minutes):
    I'm feeling angry because: (give specifics).
    What I would like from you is: (be specific).
    What I would be willing to do differently is: (give examples).

3. Next, ask your mother what she heard and if she has any questions about what you said. Take time to explain or to clarify any misunderstanding she has regarding your statements. Try to help your mother really understand what the issue is, what you're hoping to have change, and what you're willing to do to make change happen.

Once we've acknowledged our anger, we also need to respect the other person's right to respond and express her feelings about what we've said. We need to understand as well as to be understood. When searching for mutual solutions to our conflicts, we need to recognize our own limitations as well as those of others. This is our chance to think together about possible alternatives. We can learn how to face each other honestly, making the most of every opportunity to grow and change together.

Be patient. Use these steps in a gentle way, putting aside expectations for immediate, profound change and setting goals for small improvements in your relationship. If you do, you'll discover that when you love someone, even your anger can be turned into a pathway to greater intimacy.

Debbie labeled her own conflict style as the "winner" and her mom as a negotiator. She liked to identify a problem and handle it quickly and assertively and couldn't understand why her mother was so "wishy-washy." She felt impatient with what she perceived to be her mother's long, drawn out way of handling things.

During the course of our discussion, Debbie also admitted that she had been "sitting on" an issue between them that made her angry. She had avoided dealing with it because of a backlog of anger that she feared might blow her mother away if she brought up this issue. After attending a women's group that dealt with mother-daughter issues, Debbie decided to use the formula outlined above with her mother. Here's how she described their next encounter:

My mother drove me crazy whenever she questioned my approach to disciplining my children. For instance, when Danny gets too excited and rambunctious and starts bouncing around the room destroying things, I tell him that he needs some time to himself and send him to his room. He's eight years old. I don't think twenty minutes alone in his room doing something quiet is going to kill him. But my mom always asked me, right in front of him, why I thought that was necessary. I stuck by my guns and calmly insisted that Danny go to his room anyway, but it bugged me. Then I learned this approach of loving confrontation and decided I ought to try it. What did I have to lose?

The next time I invited my mom to come by after church I arranged for my husband to take the kids out to lunch so that my mom and I would be alone for awhile. I had lunch made when she arrived so we sat right down to eat. I made sure to keep the conversation light during lunch. I didn't want my mom to feel like I had invited her over just so that I could light into her.

While we were drinking our coffee after lunch I told her there was something I needed to discuss with her. Then I said, "Mom, you're such a great grandmother. I know you would do anything for the kids. Your presence in their lives adds a dimension that no one else could. But there's something bothering me. I'm sure you're not conscious of this, but I feel really bad when you undercut my authority when I'm disciplining the kids. I have to confess, it makes me mad."

Naturally, Mom expressed some surprise over my statement. She didn't know what I was talking about. I was ready for that so I gave her a couple of examples from the recent past. Then I told her, "I know you want only the best for your grandchildren and so do I. It's just that we don't always see 'the best' from the same perspective. I really need for you to keep quiet at times like that and let me take care of my own kids' needs. If there's a time when you really disagree with something I'm doing, then you can talk with me about it afterward, someplace where the children can't hear. That way they won't be confused by the mixed messages they're getting and I won't feel like you're undercutting me by questioning my decisions."

Mom took the opportunity to talk with me about some concerns she had over the way I handle Danny's "hyperness." I reminded her that she didn't have to live with it day in and day out and reiterated that I really needed her to let me raise my own kids my own way. After she had the chance to talk openly about her concerns she agreed to handle things the way I suggested. I think she really just needed to know that I had listened to her side of things and was willing to consider her opinion. Things have been much better since then.

REALISM NOT FAIRYTALES

Of course, there are times when a loving confrontation just won't do the trick. Mother or daughter or both may not yet be ready and/or willing to begin unravelling a lifelong cloak of pain. Sometimes the relationship has become so strained that a daughter may have no choice but to withdraw, at least temporarily.

That sort of solution may seem terribly harsh to a dispassionate observer. But a mother's influence can sometimes be so injurious, debilitating, or destructive to ourselves or those we love that a daughter may decide not to continue seeing her on a regular basis. In those few cases, a "trial separation" may be the only safe and sane answer.

I hope you do not face such an impossible situation. How can you move forward with your desire to change your relationship with your mother? Above all, keep in mind that you have control only over your own behavior—and we all know how tenuous even those efforts can often be. Rather than assuming a blaming approach, take time to consider the ways in which you yourself may be contributing to unresolved conflict. It always takes two to tango!

Focusing your energy on changing yourself will help to alleviate strong expectations for changing your mother's behavior. As you begin to implement the tools discussed in this chapter, you can suggest clear guidelines for setting your relationship on firmer ground. Be patient! If you and your mother have been doing the same tango for years, neither of you will be able to immediately switch to a smooth and flawless waltz. She will likely persist in behavior that you find unacceptable. A gentle reminder from you will let both you and your mother know that you're serious about wanting to change your relationship.

Naturally, compromise can be unhealthy when your self-esteem and integrity are at stake, but you can save yourself unneeded heartache if you spend time deciding what you can *realistically* expect from both you and your mother. Don't pin a lot of hope on creating a fairytale relationship. You are both very real people in a very real world. Neither of you will ever achieve perfection. Knowing our human frailty, Jesus exhorts us to forgive those who sin against us again and again, "seventy times seven" if necessary (Mt 18:22).

You may find it helpful to define specific consequences if a destructive style of communication continues, but pressuring your mother to modify her behavior through the use of empty threats and tantrums will prove fruitless. If you feel belittled or demeaned by your mom's words or actions, express your hurt honestly and respectfully. If she seems to be fostering disagreement and alienation between you and your spouse, you may need to point out what's going on. You may need to make it clear that you're not willing to remain in the same room with your mother or that you'll hang up the phone if she continues to embarrass or mistreat you.

All of these acts of tough love need to remain essentially just that: *acts of love.* As we saw in the beginning of this chapter, love embraces conflict. You want to change your relationship with your mother precisely because you love her. Or else you would just walk away and forget it. Let God use points of conflict between you and your mother as opportunities to deepen that very special relationship.

God alone can give us the grace to forgive and keep on loving in the midst of conflict and unresolved anger. He means to give you hope even when you don't see much progress. God is always at work to heal and bind up our wounds. He wants to teach mothers and daughters not only how to walk hand in hand but also how to dance together without stepping all over each others' toes.

Exercises

1. Identify your own conflict style (winner, yielder, compromiser, withdrawer, or pursuer) and that of your mother. How do these styles enhance or retard your ability to manage the conflict between you?

2. Write down some specific guidelines that you think will help you and your mother to mesh your respective styles of conflict. Share these ideas with your mother and see how she responds. If she agrees, try dealing with a simple conflict (like where shall we eat?) and see if you can both work within the guidelines.

3. Of the four suggested styles of dealing with anger, which one do you find yourself using most: expression, suppres-

sion, repression, or confession? Which one has proven to be the most effective for you?

4. Make a list of both the healthy and unhealthy ways you expend your angry energy when you decide to suppress your anger, e.g. eat, sleep, spend money, chew gum, bake bread, scrub floors, play tennis. Which of these techniques have been helpful? Describe an incident in which you took the second step and expressed your feelings directly.

5. What angry feelings do you tend to repress? When you swallow your anger, how does your body keep score?

6. Think of a recent incident in which you were angry at your mother. Fill in the blanks as if you were talking directly to her about your anger. Be specific and give examples.

I'm feeling angry because:_____.

What I would like from you is:_____.

What I would be willing to do is:_____.

7. Try keeping a journal of the things that irritate you each day. Write out your responses and practice expressing your anger with a friend. Then try it with your mother.

NINE

We Need to Be Influenced, Not Controlled

D ENICE REMEMBERS THE DAY her sixth-grade teacher asked her to give a speech on Parents' Day. She was thrilled and horrified all at once, overwhelmed with self-doubts, yet flattered by her teacher's faith in her.

The youngster rushed home to tell her mother, who listened as her daughter shared the joys and fears this new challenge awakened within her. But what mattered most to Denice was her mother's undeniable belief in her ability to meet that challenge. Her pounding heart began to calm. Because it was so apparent that her mother believed in her, Denice dared to believe in herself. That encouragement paid significant dividends for a long time to come. Denice tells the story this way:

> My mother became my coach. She reminded me to slow down at certain points, to wait for the audience's laughter,

and to help the audience anticipate my next point. When the night finally came, Mother was there to encourage me. I was nervous, but also felt prepared to do a good job.

Lo and behold, I was a huge hit! My mother had imparted strength when I needed it. From that day on, I felt confident in my public speaking ability. Today I'm studying for a career in the ministry and love to speak in front of audiences.

The greatest thing a mother can do for her daughter is help her believe in herself. That's what Denice's mother did for her. In the process, Denice was prepared to meet not just this one challenge, but the challenges of a lifetime. Take time to examine this foundational element in your own life: How has your mother equipped you to run your own races and climb your own mountains?

PUTTING WIND IN OUR SAILS

A confident woman possesses a sense of mastery about herself. She's usually able to do what she's called upon to do, and she does it well. Mothers occupy a unique position in helping daughters to reach their full potential throughout the various stages of life. When she helps her daughter to become proficient at basic skills, to accomplish the tasks required of her particular age and circumstances, a mother equips her daughter for life.

Women are strengthened when their gifts and talents are recognized and acknowledged, especially by those adults who form their primary support system. By placing a cloak of confidence around our shoulders, our mothers call us on to become independent, to stand on our own, to make our way in the broader world. They can accomplish this very important goal in many ways: by posing questions, listening with interest, initiating a dialogue, confronting us with care, and encouraging creativity, to name only a few.

Of course, no mother does all of these things perfectly all the time. Nor is it solely her responsibility to put the wind in her daughter's sails. Other people in our lives can also impart strength to us along the way. Fathers, grandparents, aunts, uncles, godparents, teachers, pastors, and older siblings can be especially instrumental. Nonetheless, mothers do occupy a key role in assuring, encouraging, and challenging us to meet the joys and trials of life.

Any attempt to possess or control another person ultimately paralyzes. Rather, mothers can enter into a special partnership with their daughters to build up and nurture all that's within them. In an attitude of respect, a mature mother can challenge and stretch her daughter in age-appropriate ways. Offering unconditional love includes cultivating the soil around a growing seedling. And we're never too old to receive that kind of love from our mothers.

A lack of encouragement diminishes a person. A woman who feels weak lacks vision for herself and tries to do and be what others want in order to please them. She fails to grasp her potential to accomplish tasks or change things for the better. Feeling like a victim who has no choices, she often depends on others to provide for her. She goes through the motions of life without taking responsibility for herself.

A person who has not been affirmed by significant others lacks *self*-affirmation. Believing herself to be incapable or unworthy of making a meaningful contribution, she often allows herself to be manipulated and possessed by others. This kind of affirmation isn't simply a matter of providing a cheering section, however. Empowering another person can be divided into four separate components:

Assuring: "I'm on your side and I believe in you."
Encouraging: "You have strengths, gifts, and talents."

Challenging: "I invite you to reach your potential."

Equipping: "Here are the skills necessary to achieve success."

As essential as assurance and encouragement are, they are insufficient in themselves. Even if we feel strengthened, we may not feel challenged. We all need someone who urges us to take a risk by trying something new. Either complacence or fear can easily prevent us from accomplishing all that we are able. When our mothers challenge us, they invite us to stretch and grow beyond the limitations we place on ourselves. However, while mothers can help to lay the crucial foundation, we must remember that it is still our personal responsibility to erect the scaffolding and build the walls.

We also need to be taught the necessary skills in order to meet the challenges of our lives. When our mothers equip us, assure us, encourage us, and challenge us by teaching us how to accomplish the task at hand, we will be able to move forward in confidence.

Denice's mother may have merely sympathized when her daughter expressed her fears, rather than encouraging Denice and teaching her the skills necessary to meet the challenge. In that case, Denice might have lost an opportunity to press on to victory. But her mother helped her to defy the limitations her fears might have determined for her, to reach within herself for the courage to try. Then her mother did more. She helped her to learn the practical skills she needed in order to succeed.

Of course, it's possible that Denice's speech might not have been so well received, but that wouldn't have meant that her mother had failed in her attempt to equip her daughter. And I suspect, if she had failed, that her mother would have been right there demonstrating ways to learn from her mistakes—another way to impart strength and courage for future challenges. The only real failure is refusing to try at all.

"DO WHAT I SAY" OR "DO WHAT I DO"?

Besides being teachers, mothers serve as models for their daughters. A daughter usually learns to believe in herself—or not—by watching her mother. If a mother demonstrates confidence in her ability to meet life's challenges, it's likely that her daughter will believe that she, too, can meet her own challenges. When a mother doesn't believe in her own worth or ability, a daughter usually won't develop a sense of confidence either.

Amy watched her mom struggle to make ends meet after her father died, leaving the family penniless. Lenore didn't waste any time on "if onlies." She simply set about finding a career that would allow her to meet her obligations and support her family. Believing that her artistic ability and love of flowers were her best bet for creating a money-making business, this young widow took a job as an assistant at a local flower shop.

Lenore worked hard, scrimped, and saved until she eventually bought the shop from the owner when he decided to retire. She didn't talk a lot about what she was doing; she just saw the need and did what it took to meet it. Amy watched and learned. Now she's a full-time wife and mother who makes custom-designed teddy bears in her spare time. Because she watched her mother succeed, Amy plans to expand her business as her children get older.

Raised by a battered wife who believed that abuse was her lot in life, Julia tells a very different sort of story. Linda seemed to believe that she wasn't complete by herself. She felt compelled to prove her worth to the world by attaching herself to a man. And *any* man—even an abusive one—was better than *no* man. Despite the fact that Linda made every effort to communicate to Julia that abuse was not to be *her* lot in life, she learned from her mother's example rather than her spoken message.

Robert Fulgham, author of *All I Need to Know I Learned in Kindergarten*, says, "Don't worry that [your children] aren't listening to you. Worry that they are always, always watching you."[1] That was certainly the case in Julia's life. She began seeking boyfriends to make her feel "complete" when she was just twelve years old. Julia became engaged to a twenty-three-year-old man by the time she was fifteen and arranged to go live with him the moment she turned sixteen. She followed right in her mother's footsteps. Eventually, with therapy, Julia began to change her self concept for the better. Her early adult years were lost forever but she managed to change the outcome of her life.

A mother who cautions rather than encourages her daughter delivers a kind of doomsday message. All through her childhood and teens, Jennifer's mother continually undercut her daughter's self-esteem and determination to lead a full and competent life. "You're not all that bright. You must work on your feminine charms, fill your hope chest, and find a husband to support you." When a mother paints such a bleak picture of her daughter's future, a daughter entertains all kinds of doubts about her capacity to become independent and self-sufficient. Unfortunately, messages like those usually become self-fulfilling prophecies.

Extraordinary courage and persistent effort is required for a daughter to reach beyond these kinds of dependency-creating messages—either by example or by spoken word. Hurdling such barriers to develop confidence is usually impossible unless there are other people in her life who can impart strength and courage.

GETTING STUCK IN THE CRACKS OF LIFE

At each new stage of development, daughters especially look to their mothers for encouragement. The way we handle these pivotal points can affect us more profoundly than most of the other events of our lives. If a daughter fails to receive the support she needs in successfully navigating the transition between one stage and the next, she can become "stuck in the cracks," never feeling quite competent on down the road.

How many of us remember the way our mothers reacted to the transitional periods in our life—whether it was piercing our ears, shaving our legs, our first date, going to college, getting married? Many of us remember their reactions to some of those events better than we remember the events themselves. Some of us remember because our mothers were so supportive. Others of us remember because our hearts still ache a little each time we recall the event.

Mothers sometimes smother their daughters by trying to live *through* them, perhaps striving to reclaim their own lost opportunities or the joys of growing up. They sometimes try to control their daughter's movement from one stage to another in a fearful effort to circumvent the mistakes they made or the injuries they suffered. Other mothers take so little interest in significant moments that those moments go unnoticed. In all of these cases, daughters will have difficulty viewing themselves as competent—even as adults.

A wise mother will deal with her own resistance to her daughter's growth. But ambivalence and reluctance are very normal responses to growing up. We sometimes go running back to our mothers for reassurance. Just before her thirteenth birthday my daughter, Jacque, made the comment, "I wish I could just stay twelve for the rest of my life. Everything gets so complicated when you turn thirteen!" I listened to her fears and empathized with her. We talked about the inevitable pain of growing up, about the pleasures she would soon leave behind, and about the new pleasures that lay just ahead. I affirmed my belief in her ability to enter this new stage, just as she had all the previous stages of her development. I felt quite proud of myself.

A week later we went shopping for her new winter coat.

And while I was busy picking out cute, girlish coats for her to try on, Jacque picked out a wonderfully sophisticated, full-length coat. Her choice was actually much more appropriate for her new image. Now *I* was the one having difficulty making the transition. I stood there in the midst of the department store hubbub and faced the reality of my own struggle over my daughter's emerging womanhood. Acceptance wasn't so automatic as I had led Jacque to believe during our little talk. I quietly returned the coats I had selected, rejoiced with her on having made such an exquisite selection, and celebrated with her as we purchased this outward symbol of her inner change. We both grew up a little bit more in the process.

It's perfectly natural to grieve the loss of one stage as we make way for the next. Jacque was losing her childhood and I was losing my little girl, but we were both coming to know and love the young woman she was becoming.

Some mothers push their daughters to grow up before they're ready. This can be just as damaging as trying to prevent them from growing up. Georgia grew up feeling like an ugly duckling. She spent her childhood listening to her mother's dire predictions regarding her marital prospects. She was told that if any man ever noticed "such a plain girl," she should "grab" him. "If a man ever proposes, slap that ball and chain on him before he has a chance to change his mind." Georgia had her first date when she was twenty-two. She dated only that one man and married him "because he asked."

Georgia was determined not to communicate those same defeating messages to her own daughter. She was going to do things differently. When Shelly turned ten Georgia bought her a bra, even though Shelly had no need for one. Mother arranged a birthday celebration and invited Matthew, a neighborhood boy, to be the only guest. She set up a romantic evening for Shelly and Matthew, including a candlelight dinner, wine glasses, and soft music playing in the background. Both kids were embarrassed and uncomfortable with such a "grown-up" celebration.

It's not surprising that Shelly married right after high school, had three children within the next five years, and got a divorce three years after that. Her mother's premature push cheated Shelly out of a transitional stage that could have deposited her more gently on the shores of adult romance.

It's essential for mothers to wait until their daughters demonstrate a readiness to enter the next developmental stage before they facilitate their daughters' entrance into that stage. Healthy growth must proceed one step at a time. The tasks we learn to master during one stage lay the groundwork for success in dealing with the more demanding tasks yet to come. And we gain self-esteem and confidence with the mastery of each new set of tasks. Mothers who cheer us on, teach us the skills we need, applaud our successes, and support us when we fail give us the vision and confidence to move ahead.

MY MOTHER, THE MAID

Your mother may have successfully equipped you for life by teaching you to strive to reach your potential and to appreciate yourself for just what you are. Even so, she may have neglected to teach you that you are a person with a life and needs apart from your family.

It's traditionally believed that mothers should sacrifice themselves completely for their children. Paying such a price is considered honorable. Mothers do bear an awesome responsibility to the children God has loaned to them for a while. Such a supreme sacrifice should never be made, however, without a view to the cost to themselves as individuals as well as the lessons being taught.

Marcia grew up in a home where Mom did everything for everybody. She kept the house spotless, cooked and cleaned up after every meal, cleaned everyone's room, and did their laundry. She was continually at her family's beck and call regardless of how tired she was. No one ever questioned the rightness of this arrangement. Instead, her mother's sacrifice was deemed praiseworthy.

Marcia eventually had a family of her own. Naturally, she felt her children deserved the same kind of mother. Despite the fact that Marcia worked as a part-time nurse outside the home, she arranged her work schedule so that she was available to chauffeur her kids to their activities. This energetic mother planned elaborate birthday parties and cooked and cleaned and did all the endless chores necessary in order for a home to operate smoothly.

Marcia never even thought to ask her husband or children to pitch in by cleaning up after dinner or by throwing a load of laundry into the washer. Because she went about her tasks without fanfare, her family came to believe that the house remained magically clean and the meals simply appeared on the table each evening. Marcia didn't realize that she was giving her family a false sense of reality.

Marcia ended most days by falling face down into bed, exhausted. She felt stressed and put upon. Yet, she couldn't seem to figure out what she was doing wrong. Then one day, this fairy-tale existence she had created for her family turned and bit her in the hand. Marcia's daughter, Georgette, asked Mom to drive her and some of her friends to cheerleading practice. Marcia was in the middle of something she didn't feel she could leave right then. She asked why one of the other mothers couldn't drive for a change. Georgette looked aghast and said, "Mom, their mothers work!"

Marcia couldn't believe her ears. For the first time she perceived the craziness of the myth she herself had helped to create. Marcia had sacrificed herself to such an extent that Georgette didn't have a realistic grasp of the demands placed on her time and energy by her part-time job as a nurse. Marcia realized that she was being unfair to Georgette by giving her an unreal picture of being a wife and mother. If she continued to perpetuate this myth, it was likely that her daughter would become a harried, exhausted mother when she had a family of her own.

Push had finally come to shove. Marcia was forced to look reality squarely in the face. While her mother had been a supermom, she had never carried the extra burden of work outside the home. Feeling guilty for choosing to have a career, Marcia had tried to match her mother's ideal as a homemaker in order to make up for her decision. In truth, Marcia was totally burned out. A woman cannot be all things to all people without sacrificing herself in the process.

Marcia decided that drastic changes were in order. She set about teaching the entire family the importance of taking responsibility for maintaining their life together. Then she stepped back and adjusted her standards realistically. She encouraged other family members to fill the vacuum created by her new mode of operation.

It didn't happen overnight, but the members of Marcia's family gradually learned to be more independent. They began to jump in and cooperate when they saw a need. Marcia began to relax and enjoy life a little more. She was able to become involved with her family in more gratifying ways because she was no longer so tired and resentful. Ultimately, Marcia's home began to operate smoothly—even without the fairy-tale maid. As her family took pride in their contributions to household management, all of them had been empowered.

WHEN THE ROLES ARE REVERSED

Other mothers never encourage their daughters to become too dependent on them. Instead, they become too dependent on their daughters. Such a skewed pattern of dependence often requires a concerted effort to change, as was the case for Carol and her mother. I could feel their despair when Carol and her husband came into my office for the first time. She and Dave were completely baffled as to how to resolve their marital difficulties because the source of the strained relationship seemed to lay outside themselves.

Carol's mother had divorced fifteen years earlier and had dedicated herself to raising her daughter alone. Carol and Bette were very close throughout those years. When Carol became seriously involved with Dave, her focus understandably shifted from her mother, who then became possessive and tried to disrupt their relationship.

After Carol and Dave married, Bette's needs for her daughter's time and attention seemed to increase even more. When Bette visited she dominated Carol's every waking moment. When she returned home, she would call long distance every night, talking for hours about her unhappy life. When Carol attempted to pull away, Bette threatened suicide. Carol felt like she was caught in a game of tug-of-war between her husband and mother. Her anxiety over this situation was beginning to take its toll on her health in migraine headaches and fatigue. Her law practice began to suffer as well.

Carol and Dave both felt that Bette had too much power within their marriage. I explained to them that power can be offset with control. If "power" is defined as the ability to influence others, then we have the "control" or the capacity to limit that influence. Carol and Dave agreed that they needed to limit the amount of power Bette had within their marriage. They simply lacked the tools to follow through on that insight.

We began the search for strategies that would teach Bette to respect appropriate boundaries around their marriage without triggering her suicide threats. After some discussion, we agreed that Carol and Dave would explain that Carol had to make some changes in her lifestyle for the sake of her health. They explained the new "rules" gently but firmly. Since Carol needed rest, Dave would take all phone calls and relay the essentials to his wife. Then Carol would call her mother at a designated time, once a week, for a half-hour conversation.

Fortunately, Dave was an empathetic listener. But he brought an objectivity to his relationship with Bette that Carol had not yet been able to develop—due to the enmeshment between her and her mother. Dave relayed information to his wife without all the emotional baggage included in her mother's first-hand presentation. Because Carol was able to be less emotionally reactive during their weekly phone conversations, she felt much less controlled by her mother. As a result, she felt less tense and resentful, so she responded to her mother with more compassion than she had been able to previously.

Carol was strengthened by the experience. While Bette's needs were still being acknowledged, she was no longer intruding on her daughter's marriage. Carol was learning that it was perfectly acceptable to take care of herself and her own needs; she didn't have to be available to her mother on demand. Dave was happy because he wasn't feeling helpless anymore. He was taking positive action on his wife's behalf. And Dave's tangible demonstration of his commitment to Carol contributed to a new sense of intimacy between them.

Bette did test their new boundary, of course, which I had warned them to expect. At first she was quite angry when Dave and Carol insisted on changing the ground rules. Once she even left a threatening suicide message on the answering machine. When that happened, Dave called Bette back, checked out the situation, and decided that Carol could respond later.

It took a while, but Carol and Dave managed to change a

destructive pattern without totally cutting Bette out of their lives. In fact, Carol and Dave began to feel more loving toward Bette than they ever had before. And because Carol was no longer available on a whim, Bette was forced to find new resources. She discovered a support group in her area and set about improving her relationship with her sister, who lived nearby. So in the end, Bette had been empowered.

We so often fear that making changes for "selfish" reasons will actually harm someone we love. This is seldom the case. When a set of circumstances is harmful to us, it's almost always harmful to our loved ones as well. The process of changing long held patterns may be painful, but the results make it worth enduring.

INFLUENCE VERSUS CONTROL

Marilyn has fond memories of being encouraged and supported by her mother. Marilyn's mother remembered all too well how it felt not to be trusted to do the simplest things for herself. Having grown up under the eagle eye of a mother who tried to control everything, she was determined not to do the same thing to her own daughter.

When Marilyn was about nine years old she told her mother she wanted to make some gingerbread. Mom responded the way she always did when Marilyn wanted to learn something new: taught her the skills, gave her the tools, and then backed off. So Marilyn's mother showed her how to read a recipe, made sure she knew where all of the ingredients were stored, and then busied herself with something else.

Marilyn interpreted this invariable willingness to get out of her way and let her do things for herself as a demonstration of her mother's inherent faith in her abilities. Years later her mother admitted how nerve wracking it had been to stay uninvolved because Marilyn seemed to be working so slowly

and painstakingly. Her mom finally just left the room alto-
gether rather than give in to the urge to interfere. Later, the
entire family joined in praising nine-year-old Marilyn's deli-
cious gingerbread.

Marilyn's mother equipped her so thoroughly that, to this
day, she never gives a second thought to the idea that there
may be limitations on what she can accomplish. Today, she's
a multi-faceted, award-winning artist.

Women are especially good at affirming and enabling others. Good listeners become attuned to the promise in others.
Women typically strive for interdependence and connectedness with others rather than competing with them. We look
to our friends and family to help us understand ourselves as
well. And that, in turn, helps us to reach our own potential.
Those who see themselves as members of an interdependent
community seldom fear losing personal power as the result
of strengthening others.

Earlier in this chapter I defined *power* as the ability to influence others and *control* as the ability to limit that influence.
Given those definitions, our culture recognizes a mother's
power over her children as a good and necessary thing.
Mothers must exert influence over their children. Otherwise,
their children would grow up to be little more than undisci-
plined savages. Some mothers, however, never quite learn to
give up the power they had over their children when they
were young. They continue to claim power that is no longer
rightfully theirs. In those cases a daughter must choose the
ways in which she is willing to be influenced by her mother.

I see neither control nor power as necessarily good or bad
in themselves; they're merely different. But when a mother
has a history of using power inappropriately her daughter
will automatically have a problem with control. And the pen-
dulum may swing wildly. In an effort to gain some mastery
over another person's influence in her life, she can sometimes behave as a spineless ball of mush while at other times

react like a stiff-necked control freak. She may alternate between abdicating responsibility for herself or believing that she has more responsibility than anyone should.

Mothers and maturing daughters must often work to find an appropriate balance between control and power in their relationship. A continuing imbalance can produce disastrous strains in their relationship. In the turbulent adolescent years, extreme stress can even result in teen suicide. In less extreme cases, a wounded adult daughter may face an ongoing struggle to get free from her past. She may swing wildly between a debilitating sense of incompetence and a crushing sense of responsibility for the world. Many of us suffer just a nagging discomfort with the balance of power in our mother-daughter relationship.

The daughter may sometimes be the one who exerts too much influence over her mother, an unhealthy situation as well. The best relationships are those in which mother and daughter are equals, influencing one another and connecting to whatever extent is comfortable for both. If you are uncomfortable with the balance of power within your mother-daughter relationship, the exercises below may help you to identify the specific reasons for your discomfort and to decide what steps you may wish to take to create a more positive atmosphere.

As we dare to approach our mothers as equals, we will see a wonderful, productive relationship blossom. We will also find, as Carol did with her mother, Bette, that our mothers aren't the only ones who can equip us for life. We can affirm and strengthen ourselves and, in turn, our mothers.

Exercises

1. In what specific ways has your mother empowered you through assuring, encouraging, challenging, and equipping? Which did your mother do best?

2. Were you sufficiently affirmed during the various transition periods in your life? What did you need or want at those times that you didn't get? What may have prevented your mother from being able to help you? Were there others in your life who helped to provide strength and encouragement?

3. Have you and your mother fallen into any patterns of dependency? What changes can you make that will strengthen both of you?

4. If power means "the ability to influence" and control means "the capacity to limit influence," which do you do most often?

5. Answer the following questions with true or false. What do these answers tell you about the balance between power and control in your relationship with your mother?

    My mother takes charge when I'm with her._____

    My mother tells me what to do._____

    I get my mother to do things I want her to do._____

    There are things I won't let my mother do._____

6. If you feel there is an imbalance in the power/control area in your mother-daughter relationship, how would you like to go about finding a different balance?

7. If you have a daughter, try to think of a current transition point in her life. In what specific ways can you assure, encourage, challenge, and equip her?

TEN

Sex: Speaking the Unspoken Word

MANY YEARS AGO I arrived at the home of a friend just as her little girl was getting out of the bathtub. This mother customarily allowed her two-year-old daughter some "naked time" after her bath—a time to run around the house without any clothes on. As a family friend, I didn't feel uncomfortable proceeding as usual.

At that adorable age when children are learning to place labels on everything in their environment, the little girl pointed to her eye and said, "Eye." Her mother smiled and answered, "Yes!" as if her daughter had just won the Nobel Prize. The little girl continued, "Nose." Again, her mother proudly said, "Yes." "Belly button." "Yes."

Then a questioning look crossed her daughter's face as she asked, "What's this?" The little girl was touching her vagina. Her mother very wisely answered, "That's your vagina. And this is your knee. And these are your toes."

This vivid exchange between mother and daughter has always stuck in my mind as a very healthy one. I felt gratified to see my friend handle her little girl's query in such a nonchalant fashion, rather than communicating a vague sense of unease and ambiguity about female body parts and sexuality.

Are you happy to be a woman? Do you feel comfortable recognizing and accepting your sexual nature? Do you feel twinges of guilt stemming from the subtle notion that sex is somehow dirty or tainted? If you are married, do you enjoy your sexual relationship with your husband? Are there aspects about your body that you dislike or even hate?

Your answers to these kinds of questions reflect to some extent the knowledge and attitudes gleaned from your family during your childhood and teens. Our concept of sexuality is especially shaped by our parents as they respond to our physical bodies in positive and negative ways. In fact, our entire community transmits cultural attitudes and values about gender and sex, either directly or indirectly.

These verbal and non-verbal messages are often incorporated into "scripts" that tell us how to act as females. When a little girl dons her mother's lipstick and high heels, she's practicing femaleness according to the behaviors communicated to her by her family and her culture at large. Later, she develops not only the outer trappings of femininity, but an inner self-concept of what it means to be a woman.

Regardless of these kinds of childhood lessons, our sexuality remains biologically defined. When we're ashamed of our bodies, we're ashamed of our selves. When we hide our bodies because we find them loathsome or disgusting, we are afraid to reveal our selves. When we see our bodies as unacceptable, it's difficult, even painful, to accept our selves.

Psychology Today queried two thousand women and men as to how they felt about various parts of their bodies. The responses indicated a marked division along gender lines. Women typically criticized every one of their body parts: legs, hands, face, feet, hips, and breasts. Men tended to be more critical toward themselves only in regard to their genitals.[1]

Why do so many women find it difficult to feel positive about themselves as females? Partly to blame is the constant media-blitz of glamorous, flawless, and sexy physical specimens of womanhood. The ever-popular Barbie dolls further emphasize such unrealistic body measurements to little girls at a very impressionable age.

But other reasons stir this slowly simmering emotional pot. Even as very young children, most of us sense embarrassment on the part of adults about genital areas. Often, we're not even given correct labels—like vulva and vagina—for the private parts of our bodies. Females face the additional hurdle of being in touch with procreative organs which are internal and thus hidden from view.

Mothers certainly need to encourage a healthy sense of modesty. Yet the messages little girls receive often go beyond this kind of healthy respect for personal privacy and begin to reflect a pervasive inhibition which may have unhealthy roots. Besides such verbal or nonverbal messages, a general lack of information may further prevent us from acknowledging the parts of our bodies that make us female. Yet, if we can't identify and accept the very organs that denote our womanhood, how can we feel positive about our sexuality?

Mothers hold special responsibility for affirming the miraculous nature of their daughter's bodies, the astounding fact that we have been made in God's image. Sexuality is God's idea. A young girl's developing sexuality needs to be acknowledged and affirmed, along with wise cautions about using this precious gift in the way God intended. In helping a daughter to be comfortable and familiar with her body, a mother can equip her to make wise choices as a Christian woman. How well did your mother succeed in equipping you in this important area? If you're a mother, how well are you doing with your own daughter?

OUR SEXUAL BEGINNINGS

Sensuality and sexuality begin at birth. As early as 1905, Freud wrote, "No one who has seen a baby sinking back satiated from the breast and falling asleep with flushed cheeks and a blissful smile can escape the reflection that this picture persists as a prototype of the expression of sexual satisfaction in later life."[2]

The mother/baby relationship provides a sort of rehearsal for adult relationships. Ideally, babies learn at their mother's breast how complete safety and gratification feel. This initial relationship serves as a foundation for future interactions with others. If these earliest moments teach us that the world is a safe place, we will learn that we can trust others. We will learn to risk loving and being loved. And we will learn to sense when taking that risk is not right or safe.

All of us need to be physically touched, especially when we're children. Appropriate expressions of affection give warmth and pleasure, assuring a child that she's loveable. If we were seldom hugged, if our childhood ears seldom heard the words "I love you," then unsatisfied hunger pangs for touch and affection may lead to unhealthy behavior—perhaps sexual promiscuity on one extreme or frigidity and deprivation on the other.

When a child isn't touched in appropriate ways, she may lack a built-in standard against which she may measure every other touch she receives in her life. She may be unable to understand the difference between nonsexual affection and sexual touching. Once she has blossomed into womanhood, such a person may be more likely to fall into the arms—or, tragically, into the bed—of any person who will give her the touch for which she so desperately longs.

Some children grow up in a family with *no* restrictions regarding touch—another source of confusion. A seven-year-old girl told me that her mother hugged her so many times a day that she longed to break free of what felt like a possessive clutch. The child intuitively sensed that her mother needed more from her than she could give, but she didn't know how to tell her mother to stop without making her feel bad. Being physically touched became an intrusive experience for this little girl.

Children can often sense when adult expressions of affection are intended to meet their parents' needs rather than their own. Tiffany was ten years old when she sensed the difference between a giving-touch and a taking-touch. She felt guilty because, try as she might, she couldn't meet her mother's needs. The burden was simply too great for a ten-year-old child.

> My father had announced that he was leaving and my mother was devastated. I knew she needed me right then, but her neediness turned me off. Her demands for affection were way too much for me. I had my own feelings about Dad's leaving and her need for me made it difficult for me to separate her feelings from my own. How could I take care of her and me at the same time? I was the daughter. I wanted Mom to help me to understand why Dad was leaving. She needed a friend to help her cope. All I wanted right then was a mother to help *me* cope.

Children need to be given the right to determine who may touch them, when they wish to be touched, where, and how much. Being encouraged to set boundaries early in life will enable them to assert similar boundaries when they are adults. If a young girl is valued by her family as an individual capable of making independent choices, she will be better able to set limits about inappropriate and undesirable touching when she begins dating. When her parents give her affection completely free of sexual innuendo, she will be clear in her own mind about the difference between sex and affection.

Dismissing a child's need to have her boundaries respected can lead to significant difficulties. She may begin to feel devalued as a human being, like a mere extension of her parents. She may begin to second guess herself and question the validity of all of her needs and desires. She finds it extremely hard to develop a sense of individual identity, with needs and rights that deserve to be respected.

Vickie described an incident which she said typified her mother's consistent and long-standing disrespect for her personal boundaries. As a twenty-year-old visiting her family home, Vickie heard a knock on her bedroom door. She responded, "Just a minute, I'm getting dressed." A second later her mother came barging into Vickie's room, despite her request for a moment of privacy. Then, adding insult to injury, her mother chided, "Don't be so silly, I'm not going to look at you! I just need to get something off the desk."

I can't help wondering why Vickie's mother even bothered to knock on her daughter's door in the first place. The paradoxical nature of this sort of interaction is crazy-making, especially for a child. It's as if her mother were saying, "I'm asking you to give me a boundary so that I can disregard it!" Then she proceeded to ridicule Vickie for protesting!

Even as an adult, Vickie is still scrambling to get a firm grip on what appropriate boundaries are and how she can maintain them without appearing to be a shrew. She spends a lot of time questioning herself. "Do I have a right to this? I'm probably asking too much when I want someone to accommodate my need to feel safe and respected. I'm probably just being silly again."

Vickie is also constantly being bowled over by other people's demands on her—demands for her time, her space, and, unfortunately, her body. She complains that she seems to have a penchant for getting herself into compromising situations because she can't seem to set boundaries with men. When she doesn't feel she has the right to refuse a goodnight kiss, she's likely to feel just as unable to say no and make it stick when that same man wants more from her.

Establishing and maintaining emotional and physical boundaries in the home helps children to know that their personal feelings are valued and respected. It also gives an important message that the family wants to protect and acknowledge each family member's right to exclusive "ownership" of his or her body. Closed bedroom or bathroom doors and separate beds and bedrooms are familiar ways of establishing each family member's right to privacy. Whenever privacy is requested by any member of the family, we need to honor that request.

Children have a natural tendency to claim and clarify appropriate boundaries for themselves at suitable developmental stages. If boundaries are overly rigid and externally imposed, children may be inhibited about their sexuality. On the other hand, if boundaries are too loose or totally disregarded, a child may become confused. Many young women express discomfort with fathers or brothers who barge into the bathroom when they're showering, or when they sense that they are being looked at in sexual ways.

In a healthy family, these concerns can be addressed and changes made. In dysfunctional families, young girls often hear their remarks and wishes about privacy ridiculed and disregarded. Or they may not even be able to verbalize their concerns. They may have learned from an early age that they have no right to privacy or to a feeling of safety.

A failure to create appropriate boundaries within the family—whether those boundaries are between parent and child or between siblings—is a breech of trust that can only lead to heartache. Immature minds and hearts are especially confused by touches from a loved one which seem bad and abusive. When a parent crosses a child's boundary by asking that child to meet his or her emotional, sexual, or physical needs, it has far-reaching ramifications for the child's future health.

Sexual abuse of children of all ages has become heart-breakingly common these days. The life-long consequences can be devastating, far beyond the scope of this book to address. If you suffer the deep wounds of this kind of abuse, I would encourage you to seek help from available books on the subject as well as from a professional therapist trained to deal with them.

THE CHILD BECOMES A WOMAN

What a transformation! When I was fourteen years old I looked at myself in the mirror and couldn't believe my eyes. I seemed to have become a new person overnight. My mother had cut my long braids and permed my hair so that it fell in soft curls around my face. I gazed over and over again at the image I saw in the mirror. I could scarcely believe it was me. "This will take some getting used to," I thought.

I was no longer a child. Suddenly, I saw myself as a sexual being. I took pride in the arch of my back, the roundness of my breasts, the span of my hips. My heart skipped a beat one day when I got on the school bus and one of the boys whistled. Pleasure mixed with embarrassment when a male teacher complimented my new hairdo. Their reactions affirmed my visible emergence as a sexual being.

Becoming aware of ourselves as sexual beings is an important event for all of us. For many of us, this awareness dawns on the day we begin to menstruate. It is our initiation into womanhood. We are suddenly made aware of the physical rhythms of our bodies which open up the awesome potential of bringing forth new life.

Ten-year-old Eloise was the first in her circle of friends to begin menstruating. Since her mother wasn't prepared for this milestone to come so early, she convinced Eloise to keep it a secret from her father and her friends. She grew up referring to her period as "the curse," a reality which isolated her behind a wall of secrecy. Unfortunately, menstruation caused this young girl to feel deeply ashamed of her sexual self.

Another mother described her daughter's first period this way:

February 14th, Valentine's Day!

(My daughter came in and told me her symptoms and asked,) "Have I started menstruating?" and I said yes, and I started to cry. It was an incredible experience—that connection, that sense of being in the middle between my mother and my daughter, and the feeling that I was the bridge between generations. She said, "Oh Mom, what are you crying for?" But I was so moved by it. It confirmed my womanhood. I was seeing the continuum of the women in the family, the pride of being a woman. I think I had a sense both of my mortality and my immortality.[3]

Being a woman was a source of pride and contentment for the second mother. Unfortunately, this kind of positive attitude is often displaced by contradictory statements from other family members or the larger community. Many women receive messages of shame and inferiority regarding their womanhood during their formative years.

A mother plays a key role in validating her daughter's sexuality when she reaches puberty. Mothers can help daughters to embrace their sexuality in many ways, such as helping her anticipate and accept her changing body, giving her an understanding of the emotional fluctuations that accompany this growth toward maturity, supporting her as she searches for a new look, shopping for her first bra, or helping her feel good about her personal rate of physical development—be it too fast or too slow.

A young girl's dawning awareness of herself as a sexual being can impart an awesome sense of vitality and an appreciation of life and its goodness—a wonderful awareness for a daughter to share with her parents. Sometimes, however, a young girl feels afraid of growing up. That virulent form of self-consciousness so prevalent during adolescence may overwhelm or even devastate her.

Ann recalls battling such thoughts one day. As a thirteen-year-old, she felt awkward and ugly and couldn't think of a thing to like about herself. Feeling depressed, the forlorn girl sat alone in her bedroom thinking that life was highly overrated. Her mother somehow sensed that all was not well and asked whether she could come in. Alice sat on the bed with her daughter and listened to the young girl as she poured out her feelings, detailing all the ways she believed she fell short as a human and a female.

This wise mother listened patiently and waited for the rush of her daughter's words to slow to a trickle. Then Alice tried to explain the hormonal changes that were contributing to Ann's runaway emotions, her self-doubts, her physical development. Her daughter felt enormously relieved to have some explanation for her inner turmoil and confusion. Understanding more about this very natural physical process gave her more courage to face all the baffling changes taking place, within and without. This mother-daughter moment still stirs up warm feelings for Ann.

Unfortunately, the onrush of puberty frequently sets up barriers between a young girl and the very people from whom she most needs encouragement and support. That lack of affirmation can make it very difficult for a teenager to successfully integrate her sexuality with her concept of herself as a whole person. A distance may develop between mothers and daughters because mother becomes fearful as her daughter begins to manifest an awareness of her sexual powers. Or a mother may feel overshadowed by her daughter's youth and newly discovered sexuality. A father may disengage himself because he's uncomfortable with the changes that come about during his daughter's puberty.

Puberty is a time of transition for *everyone* in the family, not just a daughter and her mother. Ideally, both parents need to work together to make puberty a favorable experience for their daughter. While respecting appropriate sexual and emotional boundaries, a daughter needs consistent affirmation from both parents during this crucial transition from childhood to womanhood.

In most families, however, the major responsibility for seeing a daughter through puberty falls to her mother. Our mothers often shape our attitudes about our bodies and our sexuality more than any other single person in our lives. If a mother has difficulty accepting her own sexuality, she will inevitably communicate ambivalent or negative messages to her daughter. If a mother values her femaleness, she can better pass on the joys of womanhood to the next generation.

LABORING TO LET GO

Poet Adrienne Rich writes, "Probably there is nothing in human nature more resonant with charges than the flow of energy between two biologically alike bodies, one of which has lain in amniotic bliss inside the other, one of which labored to give birth to the other. The materials are here for the deepest mutuality and most painful estrangement."[4]

Conceiving, birthing, nursing, and cuddling a child can give a mother a deep thankfulness for her body and her womanhood. This heightened appreciation helps her to recognize the extent to which she and her daughter are akin to one another. A daughter's journey from childhood to womanhood frequently reminds a mother of her own passage through puberty—a sort of déjà vu experience. Perhaps she also intuitively senses that her daughter's budding sexuality will eventually lead to their separation.

Somehow sensing her mother's feelings, a daughter may actually fear that her mother will fail to respect her as an individual in her own right. After all, they are both women from the same stock. As a result, that daughter may take drastic steps to establish herself as separate from her mother.

The toddler begins to separate from her mother for very short periods of time when she first learns to crawl. But the teenager hops into a car and drives away for hours at a time. What's more, adolescents often send disdainful messages to their parents, such as "You can be replaced" or "I don't need you anymore." If allowed, they will spend more time with friends of both sexes than they do with family. Teens typically depend more on their peers for information and emotional support than on their parents.

In the face of such apparent rejection, a mother must learn when it is appropriate to continue to hold on or when it is appropriate to let go. As she struggles to learn this particularly difficult lesson, a lonely mother may end up watching from the sidelines rather than being the pivotal person in her daughter's life. But a wise mother can prepare her daughter to be responsibly independent, to respect the sanctity of her body, and to expect others to do the same.

My friend Shirley began dreaming of romance and courtship at the early age of thirteen or fourteen. She was looking for a knight in shining armor to take her breath away and make her happier than she'd ever been before. Shirley remembers the way she and her visiting cousin giggled together, enthralled with the possibilities they were just beginning to perceive.

Both of their mothers had spent their lives putting meals on the table, tending vegetable gardens, canning, collecting eggs, and taking care of their families. Shirley and her cousin didn't want that kind of existence. They dreamed of fairytale romances and storybook marriages. As they whispered their secret fantasies of sexual discovery to one another each night before they fell asleep, every star which shone through their bedroom window seemed destined to lead them to new and exciting ventures in life.

Mothers often feel frozen with fear over their daughters' sexual potential. The potential risks of sexual involvement such as unplanned pregnancy, disease, and disastrous emotional trauma all give mothers just cause to worry. One mother described the gut-wrenching fear she felt as she watched her gorgeous, seventeen-year-old, redheaded daughter get into a car full of teenagers on their way to a party:

> I felt afraid for her. I was aware of how much the boys were focused on her sexuality and on their own. I didn't trust them and I worried that my daughter might not be able to take care of herself. I called out to her not to go with them, to stay home with me where I could protect her from harm. But, it was too late! She wanted to go with them and there was no way to change her mind. She was craving relationships. She wished to explore her sexuality. She loved their responsiveness to her body. I could do nothing to stop them. She glanced back at me with disgust because I was trying to control her life. I was left behind in the dust. I felt bad. I had no control. I wondered if my worst fears would come true.
>
> Then I startled awake in a cold sweat. I pinched myself, trembling quietly in my bed. I was immediately aware that my dream was an expression of my fears for my adolescent daughter. I was thankful it was just a bad dream. But I knew the time would eventually come when she would be making choices that were not under my control and I would no longer be able to shelter her from potential dangers.

Teenagers do sometimes make choices that seriously threaten their future happiness, or even their very lives. Knowing this, mothers sometimes cling to their daughters more tightly than is necessary. Yet God expects parents to teach their children how to develop their sexuality according to biblical principles. The best thing they can do is teach healthy attitudes and values so that their daughters will be prepared to make wise and assertive decisions about the ways in which they handle their sexuality.

In *Sex for Christians,* Lewis Smedes suggests three patterns for our sexual lives:

1. The sexuality of every person is meant to be woven into the whole character of that person and integrated into his or her quest for human values.
2. The sexuality of every person is meant to be an urge toward and a means of expressing a deep personal relationship with another person.
3. The sexuality of every person is meant to move him or her toward a heterosexual union of committed love.[5]

Unfortunately, most of our mothers grew up in homes where sex was a shameful, taboo topic of conversation. Our mothers may not have been prepared to pass these biblical principles on to us—not because they didn't believe in them, but because they simply weren't prepared to discuss sex at all. As a result, many women stumble and fall into step with the multitude of ways in which the world distorts the wondrous gift of sex.

Some people make the mistake of severing their sexual expression from their other life goals and needs. Some make physical release their aim rather than viewing that release as a single part of a marriage relationship. Still others ignore the fact that permanence is an essential component of true commitment. Yet even when we make mistakes in expressing our own sexuality, God stands ready to blot out our past and offer new hope for our future.

Within the past twenty years or so women have begun to see their bodies and their sexuality as more acceptable. While that greater acceptance can be wonderful, it also results in added pressures in the sexual arena. Most young women wish they could discuss these kinds of pressures with an accepting older woman—preferably their mothers. Yet when mothers still feel bound by the taboos of their own generation, it can be particularly difficult for mothers and daughters to find common ground.

Our current society's view of sex complicates things still more. It not only promotes sex, but fabulous sex. The passionate scenes in television and movies often portray unrealistic notions about making love. The sexual revolution of the sixties which promised freedom actually led to a kind of bondage that our mothers and grandmothers could never have imagined. Women of this day and age face the threat of disease and even death with the onset of herpes, chlamydia, AIDS, and the like. How can mothers help their daughters to hear a more positive message within a biblical framework?

PASSIONATE MESSAGES ABOUT SEX

"I know, Mother! I know! I know better, Mother!" We can sometimes become exasperated with mothers who never seem to lose their passion for cautioning us about sex. Many of us were instilled with fear in order to protect moral backbone from caving in to the passion of youth.

But what mothers *don't* tell us about sex can keep us dangerously ignorant. In response to maternal silence, many of us sought information about sex from our peers who were just as ignorant as we were. For ten years one young woman believed the misinformation she got from a friend, "You go to the doctor, he puts his penis in you, and that's how you get pregnant." Is it any wonder she avoided the doctor's office like a plague? A human sexuality course in high school finally set her straight.

What mothers *do* tell us about sex can keep us ignorant as well. The most common messages warn us to avoid sexual expression of any kind: **"Don't Do It!"** Whether covert or overt, such blanket warnings deceive us into thinking that sex equals intercourse. This narrow definition limits our ability to develop a holistic understanding about the multi-faceted aspects of being a sexual person.

Worse still, some mothers give "Do But Don't" messages. "Do give a boy enough to keep him interested, but don't give him too much." "Do be a little sexual, but don't get pregnant." "Do kiss, but don't pet." Young women who receive this kind of advice are left guessing. How much is too much? They wonder how to manage being sexual without "going all the way." They give and hold back at the same time, setting up patterns that can plague them later when they want to be totally responsive to their husbands.

Making decisions about when and how to express our sexuality is an important part of our developmental growth. And appropriate boundary-setting is an important element of establishing a sense of self-worth about ourselves as sexual beings. Openly communicating with our parents about our sexuality helps us to establish clear guidelines for our behavior in this area. If a lack of guidance and information forces us into learning about ourselves as sexual beings by a process of trial and error, we're almost guaranteed to make costly mistakes. Open communication on this topic must be established early in a child's life, not just before she goes out on her first date.

I heard an even more tragic story about a mother's advice to her daughter the night before she was to be married. This mother knew Barbara was still a virgin and wanted to help her daughter anticipate the wedding night. Her mother described intercourse as "the most fabulous experience you could ever know." Realizing that she also needed to warn her daughter, she added, "But the first time you have intercourse, it feels like a telephone pole going through you."

Needless to say, there was no way Barbara was going to let that happen to her on her wedding night. This newlywed was so frightened that she and her husband were not able to consummate their marriage during their honeymoon. Her husband, a kind and loving man, wisely made no demands on her as they enjoyed this time of intimacy without intercourse.

Upon returning home, Barbara visited a physician and asked for help. The doctor scolded her for being rigid and for depriving her husband of his "rights" on *his* honeymoon. Rather than getting the help she sought, this doctor made matters worse by heaping shame onto an already frightened young bride. Barb struggled for years with sexual dissatisfaction and feelings of inadequacy.

Barbara's mother could have given her so much more. If her daughter had learned to see herself as a fully sexual being long before her wedding night, her initial experience of lovemaking might have been quite different. In order for us to emerge a healthy, sexual person, our sexuality must be woven into our concept of ourselves as a whole.

A mother needs to define and demonstrate her belief in a Christian value system. She can help her daughter develop strong self-esteem by providing enough physical contact through hugs and touching, as well as by encouraging loving relationships with family members of both sexes. A mother can model a healthy view of sex, affirm her daughter's gender identity, and help her feel comfortable with a range of personal and social behavior as a female. These are all factors in the development of a healthy perspective regarding sex and womanhood.

Teaching and adhering to a moral framework in no way deprives ourselves or our children of pleasure. Rather, biblical guidelines enable us to develop intimacy within a loving and trusting marriage relationship. When you hold yourself in high esteem, as well as your spouse and your relationship, sex deepens and enriches that shared bond of mutuality. Without that deep personal regard, sex can become degrading and mechanistic. If we are to be responsible and accountable, our choices must be based on far more than personal gratification. We must ask with integrity, "Is this excellent in God's sight?"

What happens when you sincerely wish to please God and yet still find it difficult to make responsible choices? Investigate the *cause* of the difficulty. Do we have a clear sense of our values? Do we understand appropriate boundaries? When we're clear in those two areas, we will almost always find that we have the courage to act according to our values by maintaining our boundaries. If you feel confused, perhaps a Christian therapy group could help you to understand and establish healthier boundaries. The following exercises may be a helpful way to begin exploring this issue in your own life.

Exercises

1. Do you remember the first day you began to menstruate? Describe what happened in detail. How did your mother respond? What new things did you understand about yourself that day? In what ways do you still struggle with your monthly cycle today?

2. What do you remember about becoming aware of yourself as a sexual person? Who affirmed you in this discovery?

3. In what ways were the boundaries in your childhood home well defined? What do you remember about having access to private space, shared space, or special places for warm interaction? Describe any ways in which you felt your boundaries were disrespected.

4. Did you ever have a sacred boundary violated (e.g., rape, incest, uncomfortable feelings around father or brothers, coercive sibling encounters)? Give yourself permission to acknowledge your feelings (anger, sadness, fear) about this violation of your inner heart and soul. Share this with a trusted friend or therapist who can help you feel safe with these memories.

5. What was your parents' marriage like? Do you have reason to believe they had a loving sexual relationship? Did they model an appropriate contentment and pride in their sexuality? How did they influence your feelings about yourself and marriage in general?

ELEVEN

~~~~~

When It's Time
to Say Goodbye

It was the sweetest, most mysterious-looking place anyone could imagine.... "How still it is!" she whispered. "How still!" ... She was inside the wonderful garden and she could come through the door under the ivy any time and she felt as if she had found a world all her own.[1]

MARY, THE YOUNG ORPHAN GIRL in Frances Hodgson Burnett's classic novel, is enticed into leaving her guardian's huge house in order to explore the mysterious garden she has discovered in his backyard. In the stillness of that hiding place, Mary discovers herself.

In the same way, we are enticed from our familiar surroundings in search of a garden of our own, a place where we may discover ourselves. We intentionally separate ourselves from the security of mother's arms and enter the insecurity of our own world. That supreme act of courage doesn't happen all at once. It happens by inches. Because the road ahead seems so inviting—yet so scary—we struggle with ambivalence, hesitating to take that first step.

And there are so many first steps. At first, we crawl away from our mothers for just a brief moment. Then we step into our first day of school, our first overnighter, our first date. Each step we take seems to draw us away from our mother's arms and further along the road toward our ultimate goal. At a very early age we somehow instinctively sense that our goal is somewhere "out there," not in Mother's lap. And when we peek beyond our family's garden gate, we catch glimpses of an exciting world beckoning to us. It's too much to resist. Then in one bold moment, we strike out in order to discover a private garden of our own.

As we grow, teachers and friends help us to define and beautify our personal garden. As adults we may still be able to pick out the distinctive sunflowers planted by a favorite grade school teacher or the Easter lily added by one of our Sunday School teachers. Finally, we leave home to attend college, to take a job in another area, or to start a family of our own. With a bittersweet kind of feeling, we realize we'll never be able to go back home as the same person we once were. We've grown up.

BECOMING A SEPARATE SELF

Some of us fail to make that final step toward a separate self even when we move out of our parents' home. In pursuit of our own dreams, we may go away to school, walk down the aisle, or even travel half way around the world... but somehow, we don't really manage to fully separate. We seem to leave the unwoven threads of our lives in Mother's hands, no matter how far away we may be.

Some daughters depart prematurely, leaving unfinished business that blocks self-discovery. Others wait too long before they break away. Some never leave at all, fearful an overly-dependent mother's life would end. Becoming a separate self is hardly cause to celebrate if you believe your mother will lose too much to survive in the process.

Mothers and daughters who manage to go through this separation process in a healthy way allow themselves to grieve. They accept the losses that are a part of every leave-taking. Daughter announces joyously, "I'm leaving home... I'm ready to go out on my own... Thanks for the guidance... Wish me good fortune and bid me farewell." Mother takes delight in the occasion. Her daughter is clearly ready to be her own person and that's what Mom wanted all along. Daughter can leave with her mother's blessing.

At some point in time—if all goes well—we become ready and able to truly leave home, not just in body but in spirit. That juncture is determined by the level of differentiation we have achieved, whether or not we see ourselves as individuals standing apart from our families. Differentiation allows us to be in tune with ourselves, to know what we want, and to move toward our personal goals, and to follow wherever God leads.

Letting go also means admitting that our mothers are imperfect, accepting that they cannot always be available, nor can they satisfy all our needs. When we take responsibility for ourselves, we do what we believe is right without feeling guilty. We take charge of our lives without blaming our mothers for our troubles.

Leaving home certainly does not automatically flick some magical differentiation switch into the "on" position. We may look back on our wedding day, the day we went away to college, the day we moved into our first apartment, or the day we took our first job as *the day we left home,* but it may not be the day we truly became our own person. These events represent rites of passage in our lives suggestive of separation, but many of us don't fully complete this leave-taking until much later in our lives.

To be truly differentiated, both mother and daughter need to reach a level of *emotional* separateness. Mother needs to allow sufficient space for you to become your own person. What signposts typically indicate your mother has firmly negotiated this new turn in the road? She no longer claims your time and energy without first consulting you. She respects your judgment, admits that her input is limited, and accepts your decisions. Emotional separateness means your mother understands that the mountains and valleys in your life are different from those in her own and considers you capable of facing your own pain. She realizes that she can trust you to meet your own needs without her intervention—not that she wouldn't respond to a reasonable and timely request for help. Ultimately, adequate differentiation means that your mother has entrusted you into the care of God.

What might we look for on the daughter's part? Rudyard Kipling wrote: "Daughter I am in my mother's house, But mistress in my own." A differentiated daughter has established a life of her own, generally in a separate residence. She is financially independent and emotionally autonomous, with an organized support system that may include her mom but isn't exclusively reliant upon her. Her lifestyle reflects her own ideas and values. She possesses her own sense of worth, purpose, and meaning, and expresses her faith in God in her own unique way.

Truly leaving home is a momentous day, whether we leave in a huff, in fear and trembling, in sadness and tears, or in ecstatic joy. We have been growing toward this day since we drew our first breath—the moment when we become the mistress in our own lives. We are free to make wise and foolish decisions, free to succeed and fail, free to rejoice in ecstatic moments of triumph and to sob in deep moments of despair. And we would love to share all those special moments with our mothers, as equal adults in this grand adventure of life.

LETTING GO AGAIN

Just when we may have hit our stride, just when we may be basking in the pleasures of our own success, we may face an unexpected disruption. One day, our mothers may come knocking on our garden gate, needing us as we once needed them.

When we begin to notice signs of physical or mental decline in this person so dear to us, we're suddenly and painfully aware that they won't be there for us forever. When I first saw my mother's steps falter it took my breath away. The thought that I might soon be called upon to let go a second time—this time with finality—caught me in a tangle of emotions.

The small child in each of us seems to assume that our mothers will always be there for us. That childhood fantasy is often dispelled suddenly. If a mother's health fails too drastically, we may find that she must now become dependent on us. Pat came face-to-face with that difficult realization last fall:

The four of us were driving home from my brother's wedding when my sister and I first became aware of how much our mother was slipping. I was driving, Dad had fallen asleep sitting next to me in the front seat. That's when Mom leaned on my sister's shoulder in the back seat of the car and started crying. She told us how scared she had been the month before when our father was sick with the flu. She kept repeating, "I thought he was going to die."

That's when my mother told us that Dad's temperature had soared to one hundred four degrees. She had been paralyzed by fear—so paralyzed that she could do nothing but sit beside him hoping he would be all right. That's when my sister and I realized the seriousness of her confession. He could have died that night because she no longer had the ability to care for him in a crisis.

"How unlike her," I thought, as I listened from the front seat of the car. She had always taken charge, acted without hesitation, made competent decisions whenever needed. What had transpired over the last few months that caused her to feel so inadequate this time?

My sister and I were shocked. Our mother was growing old. We were forced to face the fact that, for the first time, Mom felt overwhelmed by the responsibilities of life. If we had continued in our denial it could have had grave consequences for her and our father. He had made it through that emergency without medical help, but the next time it could be fatal. When we arrived at my parents' home we immediately made arrangements with neighbors and their doctor so they wouldn't find themselves in a similar situation again.

The dutiful daughter usually springs forth when we are faced with a mother's decline. Yet, the need never seems to hit at a convenient time. Sometimes it hits in our middle age, just when we breathe a sigh of relief because our own children are nearly grown. We're eager to relax and take a much-needed break before moving on to new challenges. Or it may hit just when we're in our prime, happily engaged in a job or other activities of our choosing.

Mother may come knocking at the door when you least expect it. And you can hardly turn her away. If you are presented with the difficult task of caring for an elderly mother, you naturally want to receive her in a loving way and not grudgingly. But you perhaps wonder whether you can pull it off, whether you will have the energy or strength to shoulder this extra burden. And you may wonder whether there will be any relief available when you grow weary.

Caring for elderly parents is usually expensive business. Yet the guilt daughters might feel by shirking this duty would be costly, too. So, we usually try to make the personal sacrifices that are required and reach deep within ourselves to meet this final challenge of life. Just as our mothers cared for us when we were beginning life, we are sometimes called upon to care for them at the end of their lives.

Every family must face these kinds of decisions with careful consideration. How can the burden be shared? Which child is the most available or capable? What living situation would meet a mother's needs as well as the children's? Creative problem-solving may suggest a solution which is best for everyone involved. The key is to work together, to seek God prayerfully for his provision, and to receive the grace to love and care for our mothers in the best possible way.

Perhaps in some mysterious way, taking care of these sometimes frail bodies may serve to remind us of the sacrifices our mothers made in caring for us as helpless babies. Soothing our mothers is one way of acknowledging that we've come a long way together. Still, it isn't always easy. And the final letting go is never easy, especially when we may have taken someone's existence for granted from the moment of our birth.

My mother recently forced me to face the reality of her eventual death. As we sat at the kitchen table in my parents' mobile home, my mother announced nonchalantly, "I want to go over some things with you so you'll know what to do after I die." My heart skipped a beat. My stomach felt queasy. I tried to disguise my emotions by responding matter-of-factly, "Sure Mom, what do you want me to know?"

Mother had obviously planned this talk and was determined to proceed, even if I resisted it. I had already noticed some signs that my mother wasn't as chipper as she used to be, but had quickly dismissed them as insignificant. The kitchen was not as spotless as usual, the vacuuming hadn't been done, dust had accumulated here and there. Perhaps she had been too busy, I thought. I hadn't been able to so easily dismiss the quiver in her hand and arm. I felt rage and told myself I was only angry about the surgery she had recently undergone. It was less threatening to blame the surgery than to acknowledge that age had taken it's toll, as it inevitably does for all of us. This visit was harder than I had anticipated.

After taking out an old shoe box held shut with a large rubber band, my mother opened the lid to show me the treasures she had been collecting for the past eighty-seven years. For the most part, it held greeting cards she had received from her family and friends, carefully organized and bound in stacks tied up with string. Mother had added her own sentiments in pencil: "precious," "sweet," "thoughtful." None of us could have imagined how much she had valued them. I wondered why we hadn't taken more time to write personal notes, but that didn't seem to be of concern to Mom. She had perceived the love they symbolized.

As this ceremony continued, I was aware of a deep sadness welling up inside me, yet there seemed to be no sadness on my mother's part. It was as if we were walking on holy ground. She went over the contents in the shoebox, one by one. There were directions and requests regarding her funeral, including a short list of her favorite hymns and the name of the woman she wanted to sing. My mother had touched the lives of many people as a church soloist, so music was an important concern to her. She wanted the songs to bring us comfort.

Then Mom instructed me, "You will have to be strong for your brother, Don. He'll probably be a big baby and cry." She smiled and went on with a twinkle in her eye. "I want you to say 'Amen!' after the eulogy because I'll be with the Lord and I want people to rejoice with me in that."

Then she went over the rest of the items in her treasure box. There were audiotapes of the songs my mom had sung for Sunday morning radio broadcasts, a few of her favorite pictures, and special instructions for dividing her belongings between her three children. She wanted me to have her wedding ring.

That was it! Short, but oh, so painful! I could no longer keep my feelings concealed. Tears started to run down my cheeks when I told Mom how hard it was for me to talk about her death. She smiled and tears came to her eyes as well. We hugged and then we laughed at ourselves.

The ritual ended as we carefully placed everything back in her treasure box and stored it away in the closet. The rehearsal was over. Now I know my part, when the time comes. I will sit at this same table with my brother and sister, sharing this same moment with them. For now, I cherish this time of intimacy between my mom and me. I know it will bring me comfort when she dies.

FACING DEATH ITSELF

Down, down, down into the darkness of the grave
Gently they go, the beautiful, the tender, the kind;
Quietly they go, the intelligent, the witty, the brave,
I know. But I do not approve. And I am not resigned.

Edna St. Vincent Millay[2]

Living through this final stage of a mother's life can be both disturbing and healing, especially when our times together have been positive and uplifting. It's only natural that we protest our loss rather than resign ourselves with a mere whimper. We long to experience again her wisdom, her laughter, her love, her kindness, her intelligence, her wit, her nurturance. The loss is too great! Our only solace is that these memories are forever ours.

Even though releasing a loved one to the gates of eternity can bring joy, death is nevertheless a somber experience. An unexpected or premature death is especially difficult because we don't have time to prepare for it.

Alice, a twenty-seven-year-old psychology student discovered this reality while participating in a demonstration of psychodrama as a therapeutic technique. She volunteered to reenact a memory from her childhood. I was chosen to play the role of her mother. We acted out a scene that occurred when she was twelve and her mother had tenderly consoled her over the death of her pet dog.

Suddenly, the instructor switched gears, asking that we move the scene into the present. Alice began expressing her current thoughts and feelings to me as a stand-in for her mother. She said how much she had missed her mother since her death two years earlier. Now eight months pregnant with her first child, Alice expressed the sense of loss she felt each time she wished her mother could be with her to enjoy this special time in her life. She felt she had been cheated out of something she had always counted on:

> "I'm so sad that you won't be here when my baby is born... that you won't be able to hold and love my child... that you won't share in my joy over my baby's first step... that you won't be able to help me learn to be a mother. I don't know if I can go through this without you. I miss you so much and I'm so angry at you for leaving me without warning."

Role-playing gave Alice a chance to tell her mother the things she had been keeping inside since the day of her death. Speaking as her mother, I expressed a sense of loss, assured her of my love, and told her I believed she would be a wonderful mother to her child. We ended the session with a warm hug.

When premature death leaves a daughter feeling bereft and adrift, it's important that she find ways to grieve her loss. Significant events and transitions like having a baby will usually bring her feelings to the surface because most of us want to share these experiences with our mothers. Family celebrations and holidays are especially tender times as well. Talking to someone about our emotions can help us to deal with our loss, as well as help us to realize that the way we feel is quite normal. We can begin to see that others empathize and identify with our feelings of grief and anger over our loss.

Nancy was just fourteen years old when her mother was diagnosed with cancer. She was terrified that her mother might die and remembers bargaining with God. If he would let her mother live, the teenager promised she would help around the house without being asked. When her mother went into remission Nancy thought that God had decided to "honor" the bargain she had offered.

The daughter worried each time her mom went for a check-up, but it wasn't until seven years later that the doctors discovered a lump in her neck. Nancy was disheartened. She had faithfully kept her end of the bargain all those years, fiercely believing her mother would not be taken from her if she was a "good enough" daughter. Her mother went through successful radiation treatment and the family was hopeful once again.

That next year, at age twenty-one, Nancy got married. Her mother even made the beautiful pink brocade linen dress she wore as her going away outfit. It was just like her to make every notable occasion in Nancy's life all the more special. Her mom had always openly shown her love. Then, just three months after the wedding, her mother was diagnosed with cancer once again—this time in her spine. Nancy's mom died five months later.

During that last year of her mother's life, Nancy drove her to the hospital, sang to her while she had blood transfusions, cooked, did her laundry, and repeatedly coaxed her to take "one more spoonful" of nourishment. They prayed together and were comforted by reading the Bible. Nancy continued to pray for her mother's healing. She desperately wanted her mom to live.

Nancy stubbornly refused to accept the inevitability of her mother's death, even while others felt it was close at hand. She clung to the Scripture verse that tells us that faith, the size of a grain of mustard seed, can move a mountain (1 Cor 13:2). She arranged for scores of people to pray for her mother's healing.

At one point a church deacon suggested that it might be time for Nancy to let her mother go. Even though she protested vehemently, somewhere in her spirit Nancy seemed to recognize these words as truth. That night she anguished over the deacon's suggestion, pounding her pillow in protest. As she was pounding and praying she slowly began to release her mother. Nancy finally cried out to God, "I give up, I give up! God, not my will but yours." And in the midst of her tears this young woman began to find stillness and peace.

During the next visit to the hospital, Nancy's mother sensed the change. Her daughter's acceptance allowed the two of them to reach out to each other with a new understanding. When Nancy bid her mother goodbye a few weeks later, she had an uneasy feeling that it might be the last time she would see her. Her mother died that night. Nancy loved her mother and had been loved by her. What a priceless heritage.

BURYING THE DEAD

The death of our biological mothers is a bridge that can only be crossed when you get there. For those like Nancy who have been loved and accepted, the parting is filled with sorrow. Those who have experienced pain, rejection, abandonment, or abuse usually face a different kind of struggle. While a daughter may feel relieved that she no longer faces the daily distress of a dysfunctional relationship, she must also accept the end to any possible resolution. That carries a pain all its own.

Most of us find ourselves somewhere in the middle of these two extremes. Wherever we may be along the continuum, we can find refuge in the truth that we are a daughter of God as well as the daughter of our mothers. Even while we have been "on loan" to our earthly parents for a time, for better or for worse, our heavenly Father has always been there for us.

Many Scripture verses help us to see God as the nurturing parent who says, "I took them up in my arms; but they did not know that I healed them. I led them with cords of human kindness, with bands of love. I was to them like those who lift infants to their cheeks. I bent down to them and fed them" (Hos 11:3-4, NRSV). Jeremiah 1:5 reminds us that God knew us even as we were knit together in the womb. God loves us with a love that will never let go. "Can a woman forget her nursing child or show no compassion for the child of her womb? Even these may forget but I shall not forget you" (Is 49:15). God promises compassion: "As a mother comforts her child, so will I comfort you..." (Is 66:13). God promises to heal the brokenhearted and bind up their wounds (Ps 147:3).

We need have no fear when we dwell in God's love. Our very human mothers sometimes fail and make mistakes, but God's love is always unilateral and unconditional. Regardless of our relationship with our mothers, our central identity is as the daughters of God.

Even when a daughter carries painful memories of her relationship with her mother, death carries a sting. It signifies an end to those intense years which have taken such a toll in her life. The events themselves can never be forgotten, but the pain of the memories must be dealt with or they can keep a daughter snared by unhappiness. We can choose to bury the pain of the past along with our loved ones.

Kit dyed her hair black and had it cut blunt and short, a tough look that reflected her dramatic and disturbing life with her schizophrenic mother, Mona. When Kit received word that her mother was dying, she decided to make her final attempt at a reconciliation. Not having seen her mother for six years, she traveled across country to say her last good-bye.

It was an anxious moment when Kit visited the nursing home where Mona lay dying. With a cigarette burning in her limp hand, Mona seemed to have saved a barrage of harsh words and negative comments especially for her daughter's arrival.

Kit had certainly hoped for a more positive reunion, but her next visits were more of the same. Even in her final days Mona's suspicion reflected full-blown paranoia. She spewed out bitter accusations and flung shame-inducing statements. As pain piled atop pain, Kit searched for any redeeming value in being with her mother during those last days of her life. Sadness and anger seemed to mar every interaction. Was her resolve to make peace futile? But then Kit remembered that she was doing this for herself. Regardless of her mother's response, she felt she must continue seeking a way to deal with her painful past.

Even as her mother lay dying, sole responsibility for making decisions about her mother's personal affairs fell to Kit. She spent hours tending to business and going through Mona's belongings. It was exhausting. But as the various papers and mementos brought painful memories to the surface, Kit discovered that it provided a sort of catharsis.

Then, during one visit in particular, Kit found her mother in a rather mellow mood. Mona was wearing the exquisite diamond ring her mother had given her. She took Kit's hand, slipped the ring off her own finger, and placed it on her daughter's. Mona wanted Kit to have it. She received the ring, knowing this gesture was a symbol of the love Mona had never been able to offer her on an emotional level.

Very few people gathered at Mona's graveside a few days

later. It was a stark, cold day—much like Kit's relationship with her mother. Along with Mona's lifeless body—her empty shell—Kit buried much of her pain that day. After returning home, Kit spent the next several months painting abstract pictures in bold colors of red, purple, black, and blue, working through more of her feelings about the trip, her mother's death, and her painful past. The titles of the paintings indicated the progress of her healing: "Release," "Way Out," "Way Through," and "Today, I Hope."

Kit had worked through as much as she could during the dying process, buried what she could at the grave, and worked to express the rest through her art. Meanwhile, her mother's ring shone on her finger, symbolizing to her a brighter tomorrow for the next generation.

Exercises

1. Do you remember the day you moved out of your family home for good? What feelings did you experience? Did you leave in a huff or with your parents' blessing?

2. What signs of aging have you noticed in your mother? How do you feel about it? What fears do you have about your mother's death? Can you talk to her or a friend about it?

3. If your mother has already died, spend some time in a private place telling her the things you never had a chance to say. How do you think she would respond to what you said?

4. Do you want to bury some of the pain of your past like Kit? Find a symbol to represent your pain and spend time reflecting on all the meaning behind it. When you have expressed all the feelings and thoughts you have about this pain, find a special place to bury the symbol you have chosen. Say a prayer as you let go of this pain in your past. Let God fill you with love and peace.

5. Have you been able to receive the love of God deep down on the inside? Think of times in your life when God has touched you, times when you felt God's intimate presence in your life. Meditate on the truth that you are a daughter of God. Imagine God comforting, nurturing, and encouraging you with his love as your "Abba" Daddy/Father.

TWELVE

———•———

Making Peace with Your Mother

The difficult mother-daughter relationship is a time bomb, set to go off in the next generation. It is inherited as surely as are blue eyes or brown. Curing it is painful; it means shedding light on the dark places of your history to discover where you can look for love and where you must give up looking for it. But it is not nearly so deadly as pretending that there is no problem.

Victoria Secunda[1]

IT'S NEVER TOO LATE to make peace with our mothers. Even when our mothers do not seem to respond to our efforts, we can still come to a point of peace within ourselves. And that can make all the difference.

Megan told me how she finally settled things between her and her mother by changing herself. For as long as she could remember, her mother had played the role of the martyr while she had felt responsible for her mother's plight. This negative, "woe is me" attitude affected every aspect of their relationship. Megan began making excuses not to visit or call, but that distancing tactic only produced more anger and guilt.

One day in group therapy Megan adamantly expressed her desire to spare herself any further contact with her mother. But the tears that rolled down her cheeks contradicted this statement. She really wanted something different for their relationship. Megan had simply lost hope. In addition, she had begun to notice signs of a similar negativity in herself and that worried her. She didn't want to do the same thing to her own children. She desperately wanted to break the cycle.

Finally Megan realized that even though she felt sorry about her mother's many physical ailments, she could not make her mother feel better. She decided to confront her mother during a weekend visit. Megan's stomach was tied into knots as she began to talk earnestly with her mother one evening. She said that she cared about their relationship, but that her anger and guilt were getting in the way of a positive connection between them.

Perceiving her daughter's words as an attack, Megan's mother immediately became defensive. She launched a counter attack, trying to shame Megan for bringing up such an upsetting topic. Finally, she left the room.

Megan sat stunned. She had sincerely hoped for a different response. Much to her surprise, however, she felt an inner peace in spite of this disturbing encounter. Having dealt with her feelings in group therapy, Megan was able to avoid getting hooked into reliving old patterns.

Then her mother came back into the room with more ammunition. "Don't you know how hard my life has been? Your father left me with three children to raise on my own. You talk about how I haven't been there for you! Well, do you know that the only time I ever remember my mother holding me was when I was too sick to get to bed so she had to carry me upstairs? I couldn't believe how nice it was to feel her warm body and the beat of her heart next to my chest. I wanted her to go on holding me forever, but she put me down and never held me again. You've had so many more chances at love than I have. You've got friends and a husband who loves you. How can you accuse me of making your life miserable?"

Even though her mother continued scolding her, Megan no longer felt shame, only an awareness of her newfound freedom. She was no longer sucked into her mother's guilt messages, like a voracious vacuum cleaner. Although she felt saddened by her mother's life, she also felt sad that her mother could not seem to seize this opportunity to get closer to her. It was at that moment that Megan knew she had found peace within herself.

The next day as she prepared to leave, she reached out and gave her mother a hug. She was glad to feel her mother melt in her arms. Megan's burden had been lifted. She accepted her mother just as she was. She accepted the pain of their past together. And she knew that she could feel and act differently toward her mother because she was no longer a slave to that past.

Five years have passed since that visit and Megan reports that her mother hasn't changed. She is still terribly negative, complaining about the ways the world has cheated her and giving her daughter very little affirmation.

Megan is the one who has changed. Her visits are easier because she no longer feels guilty or responsible for her mother's pain and bitterness. She still gets angry at some of her mother's ideas and actions, but the anger is short-lived— not the kind of anger that used to eat away at her. Megan has achieved a peace within herself that gives her the ability to be at peace with her mother.

TRUE INTIMACY

Reading this book may already have helped you to make peace with your mother. You may have been able to identify and resolve significant issues between you and experience both repentance and forgiveness. If so, you may have become friends and peers who respect, honor, and love each other. You may have found a place of true intimacy which serves as a source of comfort as you share openly of yourselves. For you, spending time with your mother has become a rare treat.

Many other women face an uphill climb. Forgiveness can be especially difficult if you feel deeply wounded and your mother has been unable or unwilling to acknowledge her own part in the hurt. I would encourage you to make a serious effort to forgive your mother nevertheless, to whatever extent you feel able. If she cannot receive your offer of forgiveness, true reconciliation may not yet be possible.

I am not encouraging you to extend a false forgiveness. Humans find it impossible to ever really *forget* an offense. Only God truly forgives and forgets. The ways your mother may have hurt you are a part of your history and cannot be undone. On the other hand, remember that your mother-daughter relationship has always been a two-way street, and that you may have contributed your fair share to any painful encounters.

If we are not careful, our past sufferings can prevent us from embracing the richness of our present. Worse still they can color the world we create for our own children. It is only when we choose to turn our back to the past that we can look toward the future. Restoration of this vital mother-daughter relationship may be the key that unlocks the abundant treasure chest God holds out to you through Jesus Christ.

I don't mean that you should minimize your childhood suffering, but coming to grips with it and putting it in the proper perspective can free you from a great burden. When you can accept both the bad and the good about your mother, you can choose to accentuate the positive within your relationship.

Jean Lanier writes, "I am part of a network of events that have occurred in the lives of many people, some of whom are unknown to me. I know that their deaths must have contributed to my life, and that without them I would not be who I am. To be aware of this is to carry their love within my heart, and to live in a spirit of gratitude."[2]

If you can recognize the efforts your mother made to fight her own battles—even if some of those efforts were misguided and even damaging to you—it may be easier for you to forgive her. And you may be surprised to find that your forgiveness blazes a trail leading to your own healing.

Be patient. If forgiveness seems to be beyond your reach, you may want to call for a truce for the time being. While this may not be an ideal, a truce can help you to remain engaged with your mother in a positive way while you continue to work through various issues for yourself. At the very least, declaring a truce allows you to bury the hatchet and get on with your own life. You may even find that it allows you to get along with your mother and enjoy her company. Making peace ultimately means being satisfied with your relationship even with all its "warts" in full view. None of us will ever be perfect.

In Victoria Secunda's book, *When You and Your Mother Can't Be Friends*, a woman named Hannah described the process that allowed her to declare a truce with her mother.

> A big change in my relationship with my mother is that I realize that she didn't wake up every morning of my childhood and plan how she was going to hurt me. I think she loves me, even if it's not the way I want her to. I can laugh about how ridiculous our arguments are—I'm getting to the point where it just doesn't matter anymore. It's no longer the "terrible parent" issue. Now I can speak to her on the level of two adults. She's not somebody I'd choose for a friend, but we're capable of having some good times together.[3]

I hope all this soul-searching will help to smooth off the rough edges from your own mother-daughter relationship.

You may already have grown in respect and appreciation for your mother as a result of having recognized and forgiven her mistakes and idiosyncrasies. Or you may have had to admit that you neither especially like nor admire your mother. If that is the case, I hope you are willing to explore ways to make peace with her anyway.

Whatever you do, please don't simply turn a deaf ear to the cry of your heart, refusing to acknowledge the pain. Your wounds cannot heal until you admit you stand in need of healing. And forgiveness can never be real until you acknowledge that there may be something to be truly angry about. Only when you acknowledge your anger can you begin to let go of it.

DUMPING UNFINISHED BUSINESS

Perhaps you have been able to rid yourself of some unfinished business through imaginary or actual conversations with your mother. Perhaps you have been able to fit some of the confusing or painful pieces of your life into a larger picture that will help you in continued efforts to gain victory over old memories and behaviors. Perhaps you have also taken time to explore your mother's childhood experiences so that you can understand her better.

Even if you have not completely forgiven your mother or resolved every area of difference, you can still commit yourself to making a better future for yourself and your relationship with her. Have you tried to sort out your angry feelings so that you can identify the hurt that lies behind them?

Have you mourned sufficiently over the losses of your childhood? We all suffer childhood losses even in the happiest families. It can't be helped. Nor should it be. Many of our losses are simply the natural result of leaving one developmental stage behind and entering another. Even the most natural losses can be very painful.

Feeling our pain and mourning our losses will eventually lead to restoration. The predictable stages of dealing with loss are those described by Elisabeth Kubler-Ross: denial, anger, bargaining, depression, and acceptance.[4] If we stall somewhere in this grieving process instead of completing it, we will not be ready to follow through to acceptance and the restoration that follows our acceptance.

The more we rid ourselves of the past, the more freedom we can claim. Remember the metaphor of the gunny-sack? The one where we store all of our past hurts and resentments? Take one more look into your gunny sack. Check to see whether there are still some burdensome matters way down in the bottom. Is the sack still weighing you down? Perhaps you have become so accustomed to carrying those extra burdens that you scarcely notice them anymore.

Ask yourself whether there is some kind of payoff in continuing to carry those extra burdens. What would it mean for you to allow this unfinished business to slip from your grasp and fall behind you? Contemplate how your life would be different if you rid yourself of it. Do you have the courage to let go? What do you need to do for yourself in order to make it possible to let it go?

Tamara couldn't remember a time in her life when she hadn't struggled with a weight problem. Her inability to stop eating made little sense because she remembered hating mealtimes when she was a child. Tamara had been forced to sit at the table until she finished every bit of food put on her plate. Every meal seemed to disintegrate into a battle of wills. Once she sat at the table refusing to eat for *four hours*. When she finally forced down the last pea on her plate she was disciplined and sent to bed with a sick stomach.

Tamara was overcome with joy when she got her own apartment. It meant she could be in control of her food intake for the first time in her life. She was soon disappointed to find that food continued to be her central focus.

Then Tamara happened to see a movie dealing with eating

disorders. As she processed what she had learned from the movie, she realized that she had learned to use food as a weapon in her power struggle with her controlling mother. Even as an adult Tamara's focus on food enabled her to avoid focusing on the problems in her relationship with her mother. As long as she was still fighting with her mother over food—even if only in her own mind—she could avoid facing the real issues between them.

With the help of a therapist, Tamara began a new and enlightened effort to modify her attitude and behavior surrounding food. Once she had gotten a handle on the food issue, she began to deal more directly with her relationship difficulties. It took time for this young woman to gain victory over her eating habits and still more time for her to modify her relationship with her mother. Nothing happened overnight, but every success increased Tamara's sense of peace and well being. She found it well worth the effort.

A RITUAL OF CONTAINMENT

Unfortunately there are times when we are not able to resolve issues with our mothers, perhaps because they are ill or deceased. In those cases, writing a letter to your mother may be helpful.

Since her mother has Alzheimer's disease, Marilynn realized that she will never be able to work out her unresolved issues with her mom. On the recommendation of her therapist, she wrote a letter to her mother describing all of the unresolved emotions she still carried with her and outlining the hurtful incidents of her past. Marilynn knew it would be useless to mail the letter but she found that the act of writing it helped her to release a huge burden she had been carrying throughout her life. Once she had written the letter, Marilynn was able to forgive her mom. And when her mother dies she will be able to grieve freely.

Even for those whose mothers are alive and well, there

may be issues that you know you will never be able to discuss face-to-face. A ritual of containment can help you to acknowledge the feelings surrounding those issues in a way that keeps them from hindering your relationship. Or there may be issues that you would like to set aside for a time in order to work through volatile emotions. Putting them on hold can help you to gain the courage and strength to talk with your mother about your feelings at a later date.

In these kinds of situations, a ritual of containment can be helpful. A ritual is a symbolic, ceremonial act that provides an opportunity to get a firmer grasp on the various elements within a given issue while continuing our relationship in the meantime.

Recently our small group of five women set apart a time and place to have such a ceremony. Each group member selected an object that symbolized a specific unresolved issue between her and her mother. One of us provided a small box into which we each placed the chosen object.

- Marianne placed a thimble in the box as a symbolic measure of the amount of affection her mother seems to show her.
- Marcia brought a pair of old sunglasses that represented her mother's inability to see her as she really is.
- Ann put a gardening glove in the box because her mother's garden gets more care and attention than her grandchildren.
- Jill brought a harsh letter in which her mother reprimanded her for something that occurred during her last visit home.
- Tammy selected a sleeping pill because her mother seems to be sleeping, completely oblivious to important matters in her daughter's life.

As each woman placed her own unique symbol in the box she briefly gave her reasons for wanting to *contain* this unresolved aspect of her mother-daughter relationship. Each woman wanted to gain a clearer perspective on her own issue before bringing it into the open with her mother. They all wanted to contain the emotions stemming from these hurts because the emotions spilled out at inopportune moments as they interacted with their mothers.

Once they had each placed their chosen objects into the box, the five women wrapped the box in brown paper and tied it with string. Their issues would be contained here to be addressed during weekly group meetings where it was safe to process them. The ritual was designed to help them deal directly with the issue in a more constructive way than they had in the past. From that point forward, they had a safe place to deal with their feelings about these issues whenever they chose to.

Perhaps this containment ritual would be a helpful exercise for you. Take a moment to write down the current stressors in your mother-daughter relationship. Next, think of an object to symbolize each issue. What does it mean for you to contain it in a box wrapped up with paper and string? Now, place the objects in a box, wrap it up, and store it in an appropriate place.

Allow this ritual to free you from emotions that spill over at inopportune moments. Whenever you want to deal with this issue, come back to your box, unwrap it, take out the symbolic object, and spend time trying to understand the issue more thoroughly. You could do this either by yourself or with a friend. Consider some constructive ways to bring it up with your mother, or other ways you might resolve the problem. Role playing with a friend or in your imagination may be helpful, pretending to discuss this particular issue with your mother.

Once you have resolved the issue, be sure to remove the symbolic object from the box and rejoice, thanking God for the growth and strength you have gained. Of course, you can always add new items as you become aware of additional issues. Such business is never finished.

ALWAYS ON THE WAY

Mending a relationship comes through an active search for solutions and resolution. Resolution, in turn, gives you and your mother a chance to begin anew. Without healing we tend to act out in aggressive and self-destructive ways. We are unable to focus on the present when we're stuck in the past and anxious about the future.

Healing is a process, not a short-cut to health. In many instances, it can be a very lengthy process. Whether the wounds you carry from your past are superficial or severe, the process must begin with a definite decision to move toward healing. Those with severe wounds may find it necessary to call upon all the courage and determination they have in order to remain on a path toward healing.

The pain may be so excruciating that the severely wounded may sometimes doubt the wisdom of that decision. If you are among that group, take heart. You need not walk the path alone. God is willing and able to mobilize the forces of heaven itself to walk with you along that path.

When a mother and daughter can finally join hands and walk together, an unbreakable alliance has been formed. Each looks inward in order to identify and change character defects. Each looks outward to identify and change harmful family patterns. There is hope. It's hard for two people to fight when they have joined hands.

Faith, hope, and love are the core ingredients of peace-making. These three ingredients give us the ability to form a new alliance with our mothers. Wisdom born out of past mistakes strengthens us to forge a new relationship founded in God's grace.

The intimacy offered in a women's support group is a wonderful way to work through our mother-daughter relationships. Having others walk beside us in our quest for peace keeps us on track. A group can celebrate the fruit of our victories because they have witnessed our labor. They know our beginnings and endings, our joys and sorrows, our struggles and accomplishments. They motivate us to keep trying when we are ready to give up. They bring hope of transformation when we can see only stagnation. They provide us with a safe place where we can share the intimate details of our mending. They provide companionship in our journey toward the unknown.

Just as each of our stories is unique, each one calls for a unique ending. After reading this book you may believe that you have already written a new ending for your story. I hope so. But perhaps it's only the last chapter in this phase of your life. There are bound to be chapters in the future with different endings.

Life is new every morning. One of the exciting elements of that newness comes from our ever changing and strengthening relationships. Jean Lanier writes, "In the beginning everything was in relationship, and in the end everything will be in relationship again. In the meantime, we live by hope."[5]

The source of our hope is God, the author of peace. God is our ultimate security, the one who gives us the ability to envision change, dispels our fears, supplies a proper perspective, and guides us into peace. God is standing beside you to help you make peace with your mother. This is a holy venture. Ask God to prepare the way for you as you reach out to your mother in peace.

Christ is well acquainted with our wounds. He has suffered them himself. Only he has the power to bring us to a point of healing. He also asks us to take part in our own healing. He will empower us with his love so that we will have the character and strength of will to do what it takes to be healed. Sometimes, especially in the beginning of our healing process, we need others to act on our behalf. But eventually, we alone are responsible for claiming our own healing.

I suppose many of us entertain a fantasy in which we have an intimate, healing conversation with our mother. We envision showing each other all our wounds so that we can transcend our pain. We dream of a moment when we can stand naked in one another's presence, confessing our faults and weaknesses, knowing that we will be accepted and loved in spite of them.

Coming to such a place of understanding as adult women can be extremely invigorating. Yet by ourselves, most of us lack the ability to bridge the gap that seems to exist between us and our mothers. The ability, the strength, and the courage to bridge that gap through forgiveness must first grow from an intimate experience with God. Lewis Smedes says that forgiveness is an outrageous idea, and I agree. It requires divine intervention through God's touch in our lives. Pardoning creates an opportunity to be closer to one another and to God.[6]

God's unconditional love invites us to true intimacy. When we can stand uncondemned before our Creator through Jesus Christ, we can face anyone unafraid... even our mothers. Personal communion with God strips us of all our defenses and pretenses, rendering us totally vulnerable. Yet God accepts and loves us still. Face-to-face with the only one who loves us unconditionally, we begin to hear God's voice, to enter God's rest, and to seek to do God's will. May this divine intimacy empower us to go beyond our own limitations and make peace with all those we dearly love.

Exercises

1. Make a list of your mother's strengths and failings. What qualities do you especially admire? Ask about her life and seriously consider the adversities she has faced. If you are puzzled about some unanswered questions, ask if she can give you some insight on these things and listen without blaming or being defensive.

2. What specific events can you remember that serve as the basis for positive memories of your mother? Look over old

photographs of you and your mother and try to imagine the good feelings depicted in the pictures.

3. What is a problem within your relationship that you have not been able to overcome? How do you feel about it? Clarify your responsibilities without self-blaming.

4. What are some of the obstacles that prevent you from making peace now? What might you do to eliminate them? Can you keep this issue in a box until you are ready to deal with it openly?

5. If you have a support group, ask them to join you in a ritual of healing. If not, ask some close friends to join you. Imagine yourselves placing any obstacle you have within your mother-daughter relationship on an altar. Or write them on a piece of paper and place them in a fireplace or other safe fire-proof container. Set fire to them either physically or in your imagination. Join hands and pray for one another and the process of making peace with your mothers.

6. Consider a peacemaking solution that you are both engaged in and responsible for. Can you create a ritual that will help the two of you in this renewal process?

7. The power that raised Christ from the dead is available to you through the Holy Spirit. Imagine that power surging within you. It is a power that nurtures, serves, supports, and builds up. Receive the grace of God to go the second mile with your mother, or however many miles the journey may take.

Notes

ONE
Your Mother's Indelible Imprint

1. Amy Tan, *The Joy Luck Club* (New York: Putnam's Sons, 1989), 40.

TWO
Generational Patterns: How They Shape Us

1. N.R. Lowinsky, "The Motherline," *Psychological Perspectives* (Los Angeles: C.G. Jung Institute, 1990), Issue 23, 133.
2. J.R. Neill and D.P. Kniskern, *From Psyche to System: The Evolving Therapy of Carl Whitaker* (New York: Guilford Press, 1982), 306.

THREE
Of Boundaries, Breakthroughs, and Mother-Bashing

1. Tan, 40.
2. Nancy Wasserman Cocola and Arlene Modica Matthews, *How to Manage Your Mother* (New York: Simon and Schuster, 1992), 74-75.
3. "A Checklist on Boundaries in Relationships," *The California Therapist*, July/August, 1990.

FOUR
Bonding, Abandonment, Connection, and Love

1. D.W. Winnecott, *The Child, the Family and the Outside World* (Harmondsworth: Penguin Books, 1964), 88.
2. Nancy Chodorow, *The Reproduction of Mothering* (Berkeley: University of California Press, 1978), 108-10.
3. Robin Skynner and John Cleese, *Families and How to Survive Them* (London: Methuen Ltd., 1984), 246-48.
4. Judith Viorst, *Necessary Losses* (New York: Fawcett Gold Medal, 1986), 10-11.

FIVE

Mother, Do You Like Who I Am?

1. Merle Fossum and Marilyn Mason, *Facing Shame: Families in Recovery* (New York: W.W. Norton & Co., 1986), 39-40.
2. Fossum and Mason, 5-18.
3. Elizabeth O'Connor, *Cry Pain, Cry Hope* (Waco, Texas: Word Books, 1987), 40-49.
4. Richard Schwartz, "Know Thy Selves," *Networker*, November/December 1988, 22.
5. Eric Berne, *Transactional Analysis in Psychotherapy* (New York: Grove Press, 1961).
6. Laurel Lee, *Signs of Spring* (New York: E.P. Dutton, 1980), 14.

SIX

Personality Traits and Mothering Styles

1. T. Berry Brazelton, *The Earliest Relationship* (Reading, Massachusetts: Addison-Wesley Publishing Co., Inc., 1990), 75-77.
2. Diana Baumrind, "Parental Disciplinary Patterns and Social Competence in Children," *Youth and Society*, 1978:9, 239-76.
3. Janet Penley and Diane Stephens, "Relax Mom, You're Doing a Great Job," *The Type Reporter*, October 1991, 1-4.

SEVEN

The Circle of Love and Hate: What Happens with Unresolved Anger

1. Deborah Tannen, *You Just Don't Understand: Women and Men in Conversation* (New York: Ballantine Books, 1990), 43, 259.
2. Judith Viorst, *My Mama Says There Aren't Any Zombies, Ghosts, Vampires, Creatures, Demons, Monsters, Fiends, Goblins, or Things* (New York: Aladdin Books, 1973).
3. Nini Heiman, *Too Long a Child: The Mother-Daughter Dyad* (London: Free Association Books, 1989).
4. Lewis B. Smedes, *Forgive and Forget: Healing the Hurts We Don't Deserve* (San Francisco: Harper & Row, 1984), 23.
5. Smedes, 21.

EIGHT

Conflict: How We Hate It!

1. Sam Keen, *Fire in the Belly*, (New York: Bantam Books, 1991), 190.
2. Tannen, 26-28.
3. Joyce Hocker and William Wilmot, *Interpersonal Conflict*, (Dubuque, Iowa: William C. Brown, 1985), 40, 52.

NINE

We Need to Be Influenced, Not Controlled

1. Robert Fulgham's PBS Special, "Fulgham and the Family."

TEN

Sex: Speaking the Unspoken Word

1. Bryan Strong and Rebecca Reynolds, *Understanding Our Sexuality* (St. Paul, Minnesota: West Publishing Co., 1982), 356.
2. Sigmund Freud, "Three Essays on the Theory of Sexuality," *The Standard Edition*, Vol. 7 (London: Hogarth Press, 1953), 182.
3. Lowinsky, 135.
4. Adrienne Rich, *Of Woman Born: Motherhood as Experience and Institution*, (New York: W.W. Norton, 1986), 225, 226.
5. Lewis B. Smedes, *Sex for Christians* (Grand Rapids, Michigan: Wm. B. Eerdmans Publishing Co., 1976), 42-43.

ELEVEN

When It's Time to Say Goodbye

1. Frances Hodgson Burnett, *The Secret Garden* (New York: Harper Trophy, 1987), 82-84.
2. Edna St. Vincent Millay, "Dirge Without Music" *Collected Poems* (New York: Harper & Row, 1950), 241.

TWELVE

Making Peace with Your Mother

1. Victoria Secunda, *When You and Your Mother Can't Be Friends: Resolving the Most Complicated Relationship of Your Life* (New York: Dell Publishing, 1990), 16.
2. Jean Lanier, "The Communion of Saints," *The Wisdom of Being Human* (Lower Lake, California: Integral Publishing, 1989), 99.
3. Secunda, 327.
4. Elisabeth Kubler-Ross, *On Death and Dying* (New York: The Macmillan Co., 1971).
5. Lanier, "The Second Coming," 65.
6. Smedes, *Forgive and Forget*, postlude.

Bibliography

Bassoff, Evelyn S., *Mothers and Daughters: Loving and Letting Go* (New York: Plume, 1989).

Bassoff, Evelyn S., *Mothering Ourselves* (New York: A Dutton Book, 1991).

Bateson, Mary Catherine, *Composing a Life* (New York: A Plume Book, 1990).

Baumrind, Diana, "Parental Disciplinary Patterns and Social Competence in Children" in *Youth and Society*, 1978:9.

Belenky, Mary Field, Blythe McVicker Clinchy, Nancy Rule Goldberger, Jill Mattuck Tarule, *Women's Ways of Knowing: The Development of Self, Voice, and Mind* (New York: Basic Books, Inc., 1986).

Berne, Eric, *Transactional Analysis in Psychotherapy* (New York: Grove Press, 1961).

Bowan, Murray, *Family Therapy in Clinical Practice* (New York: Aronson, 1978).

Brazelton, T. Berry, *The Earliest Relationship* (Reading, Massachusetts: Addison-Wesley Pub. Co., Inc., 1990).

Burnett, Frances Hodgson, *The Secret Garden* (New York: Harper Trophy, 1987).

Caplan, Paula J. *Don't Blame Mother* (New York: Harper & Row, 1989).

Chodorow, N., *The Reproduction of Mothering* (Berkley, California: University of California Press, 1978).

Cocola, Nancy Wasserman and Arlene Modica Matthews, *How To Manage Your Mother* (New York: Simon & Schuster, 1992).

Erikson, E. H., *Identity: Youth and Culture* (New York: Norton, 1968).

Firman, J. and D. Firman, *Mothers and Daughters: Healing the Relationship* (New York: Crossroad, 1989).

Fortune, Marie, "Justice, Forgiveness and Reconciliation" in *The Unmentionable Sin* (The Pilgrim Press, 1983).

Fossum, Merle and Marilyn Mason, *Facing Shame: Families in Recovery* (New York: W.W. Norton & Co., 1986).

French, Marilyn, *Her Mother's Daughter* (New York: Ballantine, 1988).

Friday, Nancy, *My Mother/Myself* (New York: Dell, 1979).

Freud, Sigmund, "Three Essays on the Theory of Sexuality" in *The Standard Edition*, Vol. 7 (London: Hogarth Press, 1953).

Gilligan, C., *In A Different Voice: Psychological Theory and Women's Development* (Cambridge, Massachusetts: Harvard University Press, 1982).

Heiman, Nini, *Too Long a Child: The Mother-Daughter Dyad*, (London: Free Association Books, 1989).

Hocker, Joyce and William Wilmot, *Interpersonal Conflict* (Dubuque, Iowa: William C. Brown, 1985).

Keen, Sam, *Fire in the Belly* (New York: Bantam Books, 1991).

Kernberg, O., *Borderline Conditions and Pathological Narcissism* (New York: Jason Aronson, 1975).

Kettle, Julie Gundlach, *My Mother Before Me: When Daughters Discover Mothers* (Secaucus, New Jersey: Lyle Stuart Inc., 1986).

Kubler-Ross, Elisabeth, *On Death and Dying* (New York: The MacMillan Co., 1971).

Lanier, Jean, *The Wisdom of Being Human* (Lower Lake, California: Integral Publishing, 1989).

Lee, Laurel, *Signs of Spring* (New York: E.P. Dutton, 1980).

Lowinsky, Naomi Ruth, "The Motherline" in *Psychological Perspectives*, (Los Angeles: C.G. Jung Institute, 1990), 23, 133-50.

Mahler, M., E. Pine, and A. Bergman, *The Psychological Birth of the Human Infant: Symbiosis and Individuation* (New York: Basic Books, 1976).

Millay, Edna St. Vincent, *Collected Poems* (New York: Harper & Row, 1950).

Neill, J.R. and D.P. Kniskern, eds., *From Psyche to System: The Evolving Therapy of Carl Whitaker* (New York: Guilford Press, 1982).

Neisser, Edith G., *Mothers and Daughters* (New York: Harper & Row, 1973).

O'Connor, Elizabeth, *Cry Pain, Cry Hope* (Waco ,Texas: Word Books, 1987).

Payne, Karen, *Between Ourselves: Letters Between Mothers & Daughters* (Boston: Houghton Mifflin Company, 1983).

Penley, Janet and Diane Stephens, "Relax, Mom, You're Doing a Great Job" in *The Type Reporter*, Oct. 1991.

Rubin, L., *Intimate Strangers: Men and Women Together* (New York: Harper & Row, 1983).

Rich, Adrienne, *Of Woman Born: Motherhood as Experience and Institution* (New York: W. W. Norton, 1986).

Schwartz, Richard, "Know Thy Selves" in *Networker*, November/December 1988.

Secunda, Victoria, *When You and Your Mother Can't Be Friends: Resolving the Most Complicated Relationship of Your Life* (New York: Dell, 1990).

Skynner, Robin A.C. and John Cleese, *Families and How To Survive Them* (London: Methuen Ltd., 1984).

Smedes, Lewis B., *Forgive and Forget: Healing the Hurts We Don't Deserve* (San Francisco: Harper & Row, 1984).

Smedes, Lewis B., *Sex for Christians* (Grand Rapids, Michigan: Wm.B. Eerdmans Publising Co., 1976).

Strong, Bryan and Rebecca Reynolds, *Understanding Our Sexuality* (St. Paul, Minnesota: West Publishing Co., 1982).

Tan, Amy, *The Joy Luck Club* (New York: Putnam's Sons, 1989).

Tannen, Deborah, *You Just Don't Understand: Women and Men in Conversation* (New York: Ballantine Books, 1990).

Viorst, Judith, *Necessary Losses* (New York: Fawcett Gold Medal, 1986).

Viorst, Judith, *My Mama Says There Aren't Any Zombies, Ghosts, Vampires, Creatures, Demons, Monsters, Fiends, Goblins, or Things* (New York: Aladdin Books, 1973).

Winnecott, D.W., "Further Thoughts on Babies as Persons" in *The Child, the Family and the Outside World* (Harmondsworth: Penguin Books, 1964).

Other Books of Interest from Servant Publications

Skin Deep
The Powerful Link between Your Body Image and Your Self-Esteem
Mary Ann Mayo

How people consciously or unconsciously feel about their bodies can profoundly shape their self-esteem, sex life, relationships, work, and spirituality.

In her revealing analysis of the power of body image, therapist Mary Ann Mayo invites readers to look at what has shaped their attitudes toward their bodies. *Skin Deep* will help readers recover a rock-solid sense of self-worth and personal potential. It will show them how to achieve a healthy mental, emotional, and spiritual perspective on their bodies that is affirming and freeing.   *trade hardcover,* **$14.99**

Understanding Your Family Chemistry
How Your Genetic Blueprint and Family History Affect Your Temperament, Relationships, Emotions, and Health
Drs. David and Sharon Sneed

Every family has "chemistry"—the intriguing and sometimes troublesome blending of emotional and genetic predispositions that shapes each member and the family as a whole. Drs. David and Sharon Sneed present fascinating new research on the power of "family ties." They show readers how to construct a family tree that will unlock the secrets of their family chemistry: the temperaments, strengths, weaknesses, and predispositions that make up who they are.

This provocative and ground-breaking book offers advice and tools to assist readers in self-understanding and to show them how to make healthy choices for the future.   *6 x 9 paper,* **$12.99**